Faith at Work

A Celebration of All We Do

Paul,

... as we work towards our final evaluation?

Beverlee

17 March '95

Faith at Work

A Celebration of All We Do

David Johnson Rowe

Smyth & Helwys Publishing, Inc.®
Macon, Georgia

ISBN 1-880837-80-3

Faith at Work
A Celebration of All We Do
by
David Johnson Rowe

Smyth & Helwys Publishing, Inc.®
Macon, Georgia
1994

The paper used in this publication meets the minimum requirements
of American National Standard for Information Sciences—
Permanence of Paper for Printed Library Materials, ANSI Z39.48-1984

Library of Congress Cataloging-in-Publication

Rowe, David Johnson
    Faith at work: a celebration of all we do /
    by David Johnson Rowe.
    vi + 114 pp.   6" x 9" (15 x 23 cm.)
    Includes bibliographical references.
    ISBN 1-880837-80-3
    I. Work—Religious Aspects—Christianity. I. Title.
    BT738.5.R595 1994   94-22304
    261.8'5—dc20   CIP

Contents

This book is dedicated to those
who make me work the hardest,
who make me proud of my work,
who are my best work,
and for whom I am their toughest work:
Bonnie
Camaron
Aaron

Chapter 1

—Work as I See It—

Faith at work is a spiritual rationale for considering every effort we make, paid or volunteer, as a fitting and proper offering to God. It could go by other names: a theology of doing, Nike theology ("Just Do It!"), or a theology of the obvious. By whatever name, it is motivation for doing what needs doing; it seeks no recognition, reward, or personal gain. Hence, it is not "works theology."

It seems that in the 1990s, any book about work must deal with such issues as Japan, Japan-bashing, the American worker, and American worker-bashing. The recession of the early 1990s sent everyone scrambling for an explanation. The spotlight has glared on such previously unglamorous topics as balance of trade, free trade, fair trade, trade surplus, productivity, isolationism, protectionism, and nationalism.

Japanese political and business leaders fueled the flames of debate with comments that were at least ill-timed, if not ill-advised. Americans heard themselves described as lazy, self-indulgent, undisciplined, illiterate, inefficient, and lacking a work ethic. In cover stories about Japan, *Time Magazine* reported:

> Now it is the Americans who have begun suffering from an inferiority complex, a disorienting, unfamiliar sense of being economically vulnerable and not entirely in control of their destinies.[1]

The rhetoric escalated with indelicate comments about America's racial problems, Japan's industriousness and condescension,[2] and blanket statements such as the "root of America's (trade) problem lies in the inferior quality of American labor."[3]

American response was quick, swift, and silly. Photo opportunities were arranged so that politicians could destroy Japanese products for the cameras. Some companies provided bonuses to employees if they bought an American car. But with many Hondas, Toyotas, Mazdas, and Nissans built in the U.S., and with varieties of Chryslers, Fords, and Dodges built outside the U.S., which car do you purchase to get the bonus? Indeed, what are you supposed to feel about the 600,000 patriotic, tax-paying, voting Americans who are employed by Japanese companies? In the most comical response, a car dealership offered people the chance to smash a Toyota to bits with a sledge-hammer. From what I could see, no one could dent it.

In the 10 February 1992 edition of the *Atlanta Constitution*, John Head summarized the futility perfectly:

> At last, the United States and Japan have been able to strike that much sought after balance of trade. Unfortunately, the commodity we're trading is insults.

What does this have to do with work? For good or ill, work is the major effort of our lives. It pays the bills, provides the luxuries, gives us an identity, stimulates the economy, consumes our time, and frustrates and fulfills us. When our work is questioned or threatened, we feel questioned or threatened. At this point in history, the economic order is changing, nationwide as well as worldwide, and we are left scratching our heads, feeling uncertain of our place and worth. At such time, people reach out—not to help, but to point fingers.

The search for culprits and scapegoats is probably the world's oldest spectator sport. Everyone loves to point a finger at someone else, to lay the blame for anything at someone else's feet. Rare is the person, group, or society who will stand up and say, "I take full responsibility for my actions and their results." We look at the economy, recession, worker unhappiness, stress, and unemployment, and we immediately assume the problem is the other person's fault. The other person may be a neighbor, a competitor, the supervisor, the government, or the Japanese.

I am daring us to look at ourselves. How do we work? Why do we work? What is our work? What spirit and attitude do we take to our work? What do we bring back from work? Can work be fun, fellowship, or even free? Can our hobbies, good deeds, and volunteerism be part of our work? Can we bring our faith to our work? Can the skills of our work be applied in living out our faith? What if everybody just did their best? What if every American worker, who claimed any sort of spiritual or religious affiliation, was to consider his/her every effort as an offering to God? Herein is the basic premise of this book.

I have always liked to work. Throughout my life I have been fortunate to have work that has been interesting, challenging, and engaging; made me want to get up in the morning; and provided me with a sense of accomplishment when I went to bed. I am not saying that I have not had the experience of drudgery or boredom. I attended the Northfield-Mount Hermon School for four years, a prep school that believes work builds character. My particular character was built by cleaning urinals, peeling onions, sweeping floors, and shoveling manure. Even in that environment, work was integrated into my daily life. Work, athletics, academics, social life, and faith together formed the foundation of my character.

I have always had a high regard for work and workers. It seems that any work should be done to the highest standard, and those who do such work should enjoy respect and dignity. To paraphrase Martin Luther, if you are a street sweeper, then be the best street sweeper you can be.

In college I remember reading Max Weber's *The Protestant Work Ethic* and feeling proud of a title that affirmed three things I believed in: faith, work, and ethics. Later my father reminded me that the same Protestant work ethic gave rise to *angst*. *Angst* is anxiety, the kind of feeling that comes when a person may never feel done or fulfilled, experiencing the feeling that more is required. That *angst* gives rise to the kind of drivenness that can lead to success, creativity, and genius, and also to ulcers, despair, and failure. Work is truly a double-edged sword.

At Andover-Newton Seminary, I was exposed to many books, ideas, and theologies, but nothing has stayed with me as much as Walter Rauschenbusch's *Prayers for the Social Awakening*.[4] Rauschenbusch was a New York City Baptist pastor in the early 1900s. His collection of prayers is the ultimate marriage of faith and work. He looked at the needs around him in the teeming neighborhoods of the city, and rather than feeling depressed, he was exhilarated! Every work, profession, talent, and ability was elevated by the urgency of the human condition. Rauschenbusch seemed to think that if we take our work more seriously, if we all could have a sense of calling in whatever we do, then our work might make a difference in the human condition. He confronted the futility and excesses of work that do not serve God, while daring at the same time to imagine what the same work could accomplish if it were dedicated to God.

Prayers addresses a broad range of workers: children who work, women who toil, immigrants, employers, men in business, consumers, kings and magnates, writers, ministers, discoverers and inventors, newspaper writers, teachers, mothers, prisoners, and even idle people. The message is generally the same. There is a confession of our shortcomings and determination to do better, as if to say, "This is how we work, but this is how we would like to be as workers."

Toward the end, Rauschenbusch offered a rather summary prayer titled, "For a Share in the Work of Redemption":

> O God, thou great Redeemer of mankind, our hearts are tender in the thought of thee, for in all the afflictions of our race thou hast been afflicted, and in the sufferings of thy people it was thy body that was crucified.
>
> We pray thee, O Lord, for the graces of a pure and holy life that we may no longer add to the dark weight of the world's sin that is laid upon thee, but may share with thee in thy redemptive work. As we have thirsted with evil passions to the destruction of men, do thou fill us now with hunger and thirst for justice that we may bear glad tidings to the poor and set at liberty all who are in the prison-house of want and sin.
>
> Lay thy Spirit upon us and inspire us with a passion of Christ-like love that we may join our lives to the weak and oppressed and may strengthen their cause by bearing their sorrows.[5]

Walter Rauschenbusch was not trying to recruit everyone into the full-time, ordained, professional church ministry, or to become missionaries. Quite the opposite! He was encouraging every kind of worker to consider his/her work as ministry. His words dare us to "share in the work of redemption . . . to hunger and thirst for justice . . . with a passion of Christ-like love"—*at work*!

As I progressed in my life and studies, I was formulating a theology of work. To be more exact, I was thinking about work within the context of God. I could see that work is important, that it can be fun and spiritual —no matter what the work is. All work has the potential to be God's work.

The downside of work was equally apparent. Work, as in workaholism, can be all-consuming and divisive, even destructive. Passion for work can turn into obsession. In the obsessive pursuit of work and blind loyalty to its aims, God can be left behind. Christianity, as a lifestyle and code of ethics or set of values, can be rejected—even in the pursuit of allegedly Christian work.

Applying faith at work cannot be an excuse for abusing work or workers. We cannot hide abusive, addictive, or hurtful behavior behind a veneer of "doing God's will." Any theology that affirms the use of our effort for the glory of God must call us to a healthy and loving attitude toward our work and co-workers.

One of the reasons I became a pastor was that I admired the potential for a fully integrated work-life. My model was my father. While growing up, I went visiting with him in homes, jails, hospitals, nursing homes, and funeral homes. He coached my baseball teams, and when there was no league for boys in the area, he started one. During a subway strike he drove people to their work. He played handball with the rabbi, and together they tackled community issues. He lit the community Christmas tree, delivered food baskets to the poor, met with the mayor, performed marriage ceremonies, and blessed the children. In the summer we went to the Catskill Mountains, where my father was a Boy Scout chaplain. That was vacation! He did it all. I had no idea where his paid pastoral work started or ended. All of it was his life's work.

When I became a pastor, I wanted to spend my life feeling that everything I did was God's work, whether it fit a job description or not. Fortunately, I have served four exceptional churches in which the people delighted in the extraordinary definition of my pastoral ministry. I coached high school wrestlers; organized walks for the hungry; hosted a radio show on religion and rock 'n roll; wrote a book or two; spoke all over the United States; held teen-age dances; established worship services and sing-a-longs in nursing homes; led work camps overseas; coached YMCA basketball and Babe Ruth baseball; sponsored plays, musicals, and movies; formed a track team for little kids; and scrubbed pots at a soup kitchen. All of these activities were considered part of my pastoral ministry—even if they were fun, no one from the church directly benefitted from them, or they took me away from the church.

Work, as in my paid profession, has been very satisfying, but I sensed early that there was more to work. In 1977 I began a long association with Habitat for Humanity, which builds houses with the poor across the United States and in many nations. Much of the organization's success is due to a tremendous following of volunteers. Tens of thousands of people give a night, a Saturday, a weekend, a vacation, a spring break, summers, and even years to assist in various ways. Some persons build or paint; others stuff envelopes, raise funds, work on committees, help nurture the recipient families, or present slide shows. All of these activities sound secular; they cannot necessarily be considered biblical, theological, or spiritual—no matter how well-intended.

Habitat was not satisfied to be just another house-building company. The leadership early realized that people want to give their effort both to do good and for the glory of God, so volunteers build simple, affordable houses in partnership with people around the world and within the context of Christian activism. Their work is performed in response to Christ's demands on their lives. Within the confines of Habitat, a "theology of the hammer" is emphasized in order to make apparent the connection between biblical faith and good works.

Through Habitat, people work together to lessen human suffering. Motivated by the love of God to take action, they manage to put aside arbitrary and unnecessary obstacles to getting the job done. In the face of great need, religious and doctrinal differences just cannot be all that important.

Volunteerism has been increasingly evident in other areas of society as well. Beginning in the 1980s, this upward trend has continued into the 1990s. Numerous challenges have brought out the best in humankind: the plight of the homeless, the increase in grinding poverty, the AIDS epidemic, crises in schools, public service cut-backs, hunger, refugees, and pollution.

People now see volunteerism as a logical extension of their work-life and faith-life. Formerly, work was reserved for Mondays through Fridays, and religion was confined to Saturdays or Sundays. Volunteerism bridges work and faith, giving new life and purpose to work and giving flesh to faith.

This is the promise of faith at work. In all of our work, why not take the same God, the same scriptures, and the same spirituality and apply them to every output of energy in our lives? Why not consecrate every calorie we burn to the glory of God? This is the challenge of faith at work.

An example of this concept is evident in the classic movie, *As Young As You Feel*. It tells the story of a Mr. Hodges who is forced out to pasture in retirement long before he is ready. Reflecting on his career, Mr. Hodges realizes that people never saw him as a person, just as a worker. With a gentle anger and rising frustration, he demands to be understood: "You have all accused me of being just a man of facts and figures and numbers. Well, I am a man of heart and blood and spirit and feelings; I am a man of principles! There is more to work than money. You should ask if you are getting something out of it you like? Are you aware of the essential dignity of what you are doing?"[6]

Mr. Hodges was on the cutting edge of applying faith at work. As a person of feelings and principles, he yearned for the chance to find joy and meaning through his life's work. He wanted to keep working, contribute, be involved, make a difference, and feel useful. We might be inclined to say, "Now Mr. Hodges, relax. You've earned the right to take it easy; enjoy your retirement. If you have some extra energy, you can help out with some nice volunteer groups."

This advice is not wrong, but it does not speak to Mr. Hodges' own desire to keep working. His dilemma reveals our culture's prejudice about work, but it also offers an opportunity for the principle of faith at work. Mr. Hodges could only imagine that the work he did at the plant for pay could have any real value, and when that was taken away, he felt like he had lost everything—his identity and value. The idea of faith at work would help Mr. Hodges to see all of life as an offering to God. It would elevate the sense of importance he attached to family, friends, retirement, leisure time, and volunteer activities. It would heighten his appreciation for what life out in the pasture could be. It would say to Mr. Hodges, "Friend, there's a lot of good work that needs doing out here, too, and we need you."

Faith at work would also affirm Mr. Hodges in the high view he had of his professional, career, paid work. It would rejoice that he is a man of spirit, feelings, and principles for whom work is more than money. It would celebrate the essential dignity he found in going to work each day and doing a good job. It would say, "Mr. Hodges, in whatever way you can best serve God with your abilities and interest, go for it!"

Faith at work crosses time and space. It is not limited to a job site; nor is it meant only for those whose work is overtly committed to Christ or, at the other extreme, done only for pay. It merely takes all that a person does and offers the perspective that it can be done for the glory of God. Young or old, paid or volunteer, professional career or retirement activity, sacred or secular, for profit or for fun—every ounce of energy offered to God is a theological statement. Scripture and sermons, church and religion, and worship and theology come to life in a practical expression of God's love. There is no limit to where or when this can happen or who can take part.

When I first started preaching about the biblical principles of work across America and around the world, I was guilty of too narrowly focusing on what people can do with free time in volunteer efforts. I persuaded thousands of people to put their spare time to use as God's partners in good works. Through scripture, prayer, and devotions, I sought to turn volunteer opportunities into sacred time, volunteer work sites into sacred space, and volunteer activity into sacred work.

The real power of the biblical principle of work is in the possibility of applying it throughout our daily lives. We are inclined to view weekends and vacations as leisure time or fun time for secular activity. Meanwhile, our paid work is in the world, of the world, serving "mammon." Such a worldview leaves precious little time for God, unless we can turn it all over to God.

In Jesus' first miracle, he turned water into wine. He changed something that was mundane into something very special. Thanks to the involvement of Jesus, something very ordinary became extraordinary. Faith at work can re-create that miracle every day of our lives. Through the presence of Christ, all of our time becomes sacred time, any place we are becomes sacred space, and all of our efforts become sacred work. The "water" of our daily lives (which may be drudgery, duty, routine, boredom, secular, or paid) becomes the "wine" of joyous, meaningful, and holy effort. Everything else remains the same, but somehow the taste is different. We may continue in the same place with the same people doing the same thing, but with Christ in the middle, it becomes better. This is faith at work: bringing God to bear on every activity of our lives.

When I think back over my adult working career, I remember many special moments when God seemed to be using my work. Some of these are obvious: a counseling visit that saved a marriage, a sermon that changed a person's whole life, a youth group conference that led over fifty persons to be baptized, a Bible study series that increased people's understanding of God, and a funeral that left everyone confident in the Resurrection.

These are the expected fruits of my labor as a pastor. The job description is rather clear-cut: I am expected to lead worship, deliver uplifting sermons, teach the Bible, conduct weddings and funerals, inspire young people, interact with various boards and committees, visit the sick and elderly, and help people to a personal relationship with God. This is my assigned work—what I get paid for, what is expected of me. When people ask me what I do for a living, I answer, "I am a pastor," and people have a rather consistent view of what I do.

The best work I have done, however, would not fit into a standard job description, nor would it usually be thought of as work. It was volunteer coaching of community sports teams while our son was growing up. I coached two years for a track club and several years for YMCA basketball and every kind of baseball. I even coached a year of soccer (about which I knew nothing). Like many parents, I wanted to help out, do my part, keep the leagues going, give the youngsters some fun and good memories.

One year was special. The tools of a volunteer and the opportunity to serve God were undeniably linked. The whole season was an intentional offering to God. It was a season-long experiment in which God's love, God's ideas, God's commitment, and every other quality of God from discipline to patience became as basic to our team life as the fundamentals of baseball. For one season every time at bat, practice, game, pitch, and catch was a living lesson about God.

My son, Aaron, was fourteen years-old and played on the Phillies team of the older division of our city's Babe Ruth League. As the coach, my job was to draft the players, and I will admit that we accumulated an unusual group. We had lived in the community for six years, and I coached each year, so I knew the boys. The selections I made were based overtly on the desire to serve God by helping some particular young men. They were loud, cocky, unconventional, and, to some others, unmanageable. These boys were a cross-section of all the problems that could ever face youngsters.

After I announced my draft picks, one friend said, "You're crazy." Another friend said, "God bless you; you're gonna need it!" But I wanted a chance to do with a baseball team what Jesus did in his own ministry and what he challenged us to do. I wanted to gather a motley crew, taken from the highways and byways—the people often ignored or unwanted—and bring out the best in them. I wanted them to see their capabilities and take the lessons they learned into the rest of their lives.

We started the season before the other teams. We practiced earlier, stayed later, and worked harder. We talked a lot, and I taught a lot. I monitored the boys' grades and personal lives. We constantly made a connection between baseball and life. We used everybody, took risks, and never quit trying. The players were not born the best, but they became the best by a commitment to do their best. My coaching did not make it happen. I only offered a biblical vision of what God is willing to do with those who are willing to try, and the boys bought into the vision.

To be honest, this baseball team interfaced with my work, at least as most people would define work. For example, the highlight of every spring at our church was the annual banquet hosted by our adult classes and the Women's Federation. In that particular year I arranged for a friend, Dr. Timothy Johnson of *ABC News,* to be the speaker. The turnout was the largest in years; the place was full. I was not there, however. We had a night game, so I made a brief tape recording and left it on my plate to be played at the appropriate time.

Later in the year the league had to schedule our team for a Sunday morning game. Rain-outs had wreaked havoc with the schedule, and there was no other choice. It was a very important game against the team ahead of us. I arranged for someone to teach my Sunday School class and for someone to lead worship, hoping I would get back to church in time to preach. Then I told our team to win and win fast. The team won and kept on winning. We became champions on and off the field.

Now here is the important part. I am not saying that baseball is more important than Sunday School, or that winning is more important than worship, but I am saying that my best work that year was on a ball field. I continued to preach, teach, baptize, and be a pastor. It was a good professional year in my paid career, but God took the rest of my time and made it the best of my time.

When the season was over, and we had won it all, a man came up to me in the grocery store and said, "Listen, I just have one question. Whoever decided to draft that bunch of prima donna juvenile delinquent dead beats? And how on earth did you ever win with them?" I answered, "That's two questions," I said, "and that's the whole point." I left him still puzzled.

My team *was* a tough and unusual bunch. The man in the grocery store did not know how difficult life had been for some of the boys. But God took my energies as a volunteer coach and their efforts as teenagers at leisure and made an experience that has continued to shape those lives. The lesson is not that they won, but that faith was applied to work, lifting a mundane, secular, volunteer experience into a spiritual lesson for life. It is also an affirmation that all we do is worthy of God's presence—if we will only invite, seek, and welcome God's presence.

Endnotes

[1]Lance Morrow, "Japan in the Mind of America," *Time*, 10 February 1992, 17.

[2]Ibid., 19, 21.

[3]Lance Hillebrand, "America in the Mind of Japan," *Time*, 10 February 1992, 21, 22.

[4]Walter Rauschenbusch, *Prayers for the Social Awakening* (Boston: Pilgrim Press, 1909).

[5]Ibid., 117.

[6]*As Young as You Feel*, prod. and dir. Harmon Jones, 77 min., TCF, 1951.

Chapter 2

—Work as Sacred—

If the biblical principles of work are ever to be worthy of being capitalized, written about, and studied in seminaries, then we must first take seriously the sacredness of work. To say that work is sacred is to say that our sweat, energy, and effort can be important to God. If work is sacred, then our skills, abilities, and talents can be appropriate offerings to God and creative acts of worship. It does not matter if these efforts and skills are utilized for pay or as a volunteer, on the job or on the weekend, or as a career or hobby. If God is the author of our abilities, and if our abilities are offered to God, then all work is sacred.

Consider the evolution of the word vocation. Coming from Latin, it literally means "calling." People used to think of their work as a calling, or an assignment from God. The early rationale for the caste system in Hinduism was that people were preordained to be born into certain categories, and with those categories came certain jobs. One's work was not the result of an aptitude test, but the birthright (or birth-curse). Western civilization was not much different. Carpenters begat carpenters, farmers begat farmers, merchants begat merchants, royalty begat royalty, and serfs begat serfs. People assumed they had their place, a God-given place.

A narrower view of vocation emerged when it was applied only to those who entered the organized, ordained clergy. Conferences on vocations are still held to encourage people to consider a career in the professional ministry. In some circles, vocation and clergy are synonymous. People cannot help but have the impression that only the ordained, professional clergy can have a "calling" from God, and that everyone else just has a job. Such a view nicely elevates the clergy while at the same time denigrates and devalues the work of most people.

At the other extreme, we find that in popular usage, vocation has become just another word for job. Therefore, we have vocational training, vocational counseling, and vocational schools. These activities do not pretend to have anything to do with preparing persons to know God's will for their lives, but have everything to do with getting people ready for the job market. In such settings, vocation means work only. One's vocation/work is the nine-to-five job, Monday through Friday; it is what one is paid for doing; it is what puts food on the table and pays the bills; it is what one *must* do.

The opposite of this view of vocation is the word avocation. Avocation is our word for hobby—what we do for fun, what we choose to do with our energy when we do not have to do anything else. It is less important than work, but more fun than work. Whichever way we look at it, in modern usage, vocation has become compartmentalized. It is considered either the work of the clergy or what people do for a living because they must.

I wonder if work cannot be reintegrated into our whole life and being. Is it possible for us to look at our vocation as everything we do—every bit of effort, energy, and "oomph" we expend—and as an offering to God? Certainly the Bible gives the impression that everything we do should be done to the glory of God. Even the trees clap their branches (Isa 55:12), the oceans lift their voices (Ps 93:3), the meadows and valleys shout for joy (Ps 98:8), and the mountains and forests burst into song (Isa 44:23). Can we, God's people, do any less?

As a kid I used to love to hear Tennessee Ernie Ford sing "Sixteen Tons":

> You load sixteen tons and what do you get?
> Another day older and deeper in debt.
> Saint Peter don't you call me 'cause I can't go.
> I owe my soul to the company store.[1]

We may certainly owe a large debt and have to work to pay our bills, but we cannot let ourselves believe that we owe our soul to our job. We belong to God—lock, stock, and barrel. As God's people, we should tackle every job, assignment, and task that is given to us. We should be valued workers and prized employees because we give our best to the glory of God. With this attitude, our work becomes an extension of ourselves, our faith, and who we are. The same qualities that define our Christian character should be obvious in our work.

I am not advocating the popular heresy, "We are what we do." In no way should people be defined by their paid job. Rather, our essence is something we should bring to our work, not something we gain from our work. How we do our work and use our energy should be defined by who we really are. Who we really are should not be defined by our work.

When Moses was confronted by God in the burning bush (Exod 3: 1-14), God offered this self-description as a name: "I Am that I Am." This statement is not a theological riddle. God simply did not want to be defined, categorized, or confined by saying, "I am this or that." God does not choose to be limited by any description or boundary of time and space. God is what God is.

Why not emulate this idea in our own lives? Why not so thoroughly integrate our faith and work lives that they are indistinguishable from one another? Add play, family, and school to the list, and imagine the possibilities of a life lived in harmony and unity to such a degree that work is fun, family is play, religion is work, and education is spiritual.

It should not matter if we are at the office getting paid, in the yard raking leaves, helping at a soup kitchen, on the ball field coaching youngsters, in a classroom teaching Sunday School, or in the basement working on a project. Each of these activities requires our effort, energy, and expertise. Why not give them our best? Why not treat every output from ourselves as important to God, as an offering to our God, as sacred? Whether with a computer or a hammer, a ladle or a paint brush, free time or paid, vocation or avocation, let it stand as our witness to God's presence in our lives.

Bryan Adams' popular song offers this intriguing promise: "Everything I do, I do it for you." On a personal level, such a promise is romantic. On a spiritual level, this promise would be a tremendous statement of faith, a dynamic theology. Imagine, everything we do, we do for *You* (yes a capital Y)! Then all of our work would be sacred.

We have a hard time looking at work as sacred, however. Work may be necessary, a drudgery, or what is expected. A popular bumper sticker tries to put a smile on the drudgery of work: "I owe, I owe, so off to work I go!" We work to pay bills; we do not want to be on the dole, so we put up with boredom.

I was once told there are two approaches or attitudes to work: (1) We can work Monday through Friday for the satisfaction it provides Monday through Friday, or (2) we can work all week for the satisfaction it provides on the weekend. In other words, we can rejoice and find meaning in the work itself, or we can take pleasure in what we can afford to do on weekends because of the money we earn during the week. Why not turn all of work into something vital, exciting, spiritual, and sacred? Why not consecrate every ounce of energy we expend to the glory of God?

Some people can easily see the work they do on the job as important because they are paid to do it. Others view teaching Sunday School or helping the poor as important because these tasks are directly related to serving God. The scriptures, however, tend to look at every moment, endeavor, and aspect of our lives as God's business. This is the God who has the hairs of our head numbered, (Matt 10:30), who lays claim to the earth and the fullness thereof (Ps 24:1), who tells us that we are judged by our thoughts as well as our actions (Matt 5:27ff.), and who demands that we be "instant in and out of season" (2 Tim 4:2). With God there is no weekday or weekend, time on or time off, secular or sacred. All of our lives, our time and work, are God's domain.

We need to elevate our personal view of every effort we make to help us to feel that everything we do is important to God. If we can look at life this way, then we will have a healthier view of how we spend our time: as wage-earners and volunteers, at work and play, in retirement or at the office, and with our spare time or career.

The most obvious application of work theology is voluntary service. Such service is a ministry that uses the skills of many volunteers who are convinced that what they do with their free time, retirement, spring break, summer vacation, or Saturday is a spiritual issue or sacred matter. Their effort is religious exercise: It is meant to be worshipful; it is an offering; it has theological importance; it has to do with God.

The connection is obvious for volunteers in many overtly Christ-centered or faith-based activities. The opportunity and spiritual significance are missed by most people. For too many people, work is drudgery to be endured, and volunteerism is a chore to be avoided. The real challenge is to change our thinking/attitude about all work, beginning with what we do because we have to. To do so, we need to think about the meaning of work, why we do it, how it makes us feel, and what we desire from it.

Studs Terkel is a sort of cultural anthropologist, studying America through interviews with a broad spectrum of people. In his book, *Working*,[2] Terkel interviewed every imaginable kind of worker: farmer, heavy equipment operator, stewardess, actor, hooker, garbage man, policeman, janitor, welder, bus driver, writer, waiter, professor, stockbroker, athlete, musician, nurse, priest, poet. These persons expressed the full range of emotions: from pride in their work to frustration with the boss, from regret to envy, from resignation to determination.

One man, speaking from experience in the corporate world, said to Terkel,

> The corporation is a jungle. It's exciting. You're thrown in on your own and you're constantly battling to survive. When you learn to survive, the game is to become the conqueror, the leader.[3]

Barbara Terwilliger, with a variety of work experience, said,

> Everyone needs to feel they have a place in the world. It would be unbearable not to. I don't like to feel superfluous. One needs to be needed. Love doesn't suffice. It doesn't fill up enough hours. I don't mean there must be activity for activity's sake. I don't mean obsessive, empty moving around. I mean creating something now. Human beings must work to create some coherence. You do it only through work and through love. And you can only count on work.[4]

Terkel also interviewed a publisher whose views of work changed dramatically when he became a Christian:

> I was never afraid of working. I always enjoyed the reward. I don't believe the answer lies in making money. It didn't for me. I couldn't understand why I wasn't happy. Happiness is not related to money. Being successful at what you're doing is the measure of a man, standing on his own two feet . . . without leaning on other people.
>
> My quest I have already found . . . in the Bible. I heard that God had a plan for every human being and I could have a direct contact with God through Jesus Christ. I asked Christ to come into my life. My life really became worth living.
>
> Before I accepted Christ, I didn't feel I had a good deal until I really crushed a guy.
>
> Each man has a calling. The gifts God has given me is to become a businessman. To be able to organize, to sell, to understand figures. I want to use those gifts for the glory of God. I don't want to do anything in my business life that would shame my savior.
>
> Everything I do in business must be above board—must be something I can face God with once I appear before Him after I die.[5]

This publisher experienced a dramatic change. He once viewed the purpose of work as money, and the method as crushing the other guy.

Through Christ, the publisher discovered a sense of purpose, a calling, and a set of ethics. Now he wants a life that honors God and mirrors Christ. In Christian circles we often hear of people offering their lives to Christ. This is a noble generality, but it may be more valuable to make our offerings more specific. The publisher was offering his work and workstyle to the glory of God.

Terkel commented on his findings:

> This book, being about work, is, by its very nature, about violence —to the spirit as well as to the body. It is, above all (or beneath all), about daily humiliations. To survive the day is triumph enough for the walking wounded among the great many of us.
>
> It is about a search, too, for daily meaning as well as daily bread, for recognition as well as cash, for astonishment rather than torpor; in short, for a sort of life rather than a Monday through Friday sort of dying. Perhaps immortality, too, is part of the quest. To be remembered was the wish, spoken and unspoken, of the heroes and heroines of this book.[6]

This is powerful stuff, but then, work is a powerful subject. It is the only activity we can do for eight to ten hours a day for five to seven days a week. We do not eat or worship that much, nor can we participate in our favorite game or physical activity so much. Allegedly, we do this working because we must. Yet, when some people can no longer work, they give up on life and even die. Others, who could afford not to work, choose to keep working. Work is powerful stuff.

Terkel says that work is violence and humiliation, that just to endure it is a victory. He also affirms that work is about meaning, life, and even immortality. One worker says that the goal of work is to conquer, while the other calls it better than love and more reliable.

Work is obviously many things to many people. But can we say that work is sacred? Can we actually believe that work is special to God? It seems that we prefer to think of everything in terms of a dichotomy. Things are either sacred or profane, sacred or mundane, sacred or secular. A different worldview suggests that everything is sacred, everything is important to God, and everything has a possibility of being holy to God.

During a visit to Zaire in central Africa, I had the joy of seeing first hand the work of agricultural missions. American Baptist missionary Gene Gentry put me on the back of his motorcycle and off we went into the bush country. He took me to a small farm that has been transformed from subsistence farming to a thriving enterprise simply by taking a different approach to work. Gentry had enticed the farmer, Mankwela, into trying new ways of caring for chickens and crops. Simply stated, Gentry had convinced Mankwela that the farmer, the farm, the farmer's family, the farm animals, and the farm's crops were all interrelated.

This must have struck a responsive chord in Mankwela, touching something that he already believed. Later that day we had refreshments. We sat in a circle outside the family hut. A young boy was summoned and told to climb a nearby palm tree. Soon he returned with a gourd filled with palm wine. Our glasses were filled, but just before we drank I noticed that the Zairians spilled some of their palm wine quite purposely onto the ground. They were returning to the earth and to the God of the earth an offering. They understood that the palm wine came from the palm tree that came from the earth, and that God was God of all! Their efforts at cultivating the palm tree, tapping it, and even the athletic effort of climbing it and the fellowship enjoyed in drinking the palm wine were not separate from God. All of these were spiritual activities.

Gene Gentry tapped into the idea of unity and harmony of all activity when he agreed to work with Mankwela. Mankwela was taught not just to own chickens but to care for the chickens, not just to plant but to plant according to the terrain, and not just to harvest but to prune. As a result, Mankwela learned not just to subsist but to prosper, and not just to avoid starvation but to be able to send his children to school. Life went from despair to enjoyment. Work went from drudgery to something of which he could be proud, and God was the center of it all. The missionary servant to God tapped into the African's traditional understanding of God to reaffirm that all of life is activity connected and related to God. Mankwela had known to make an offering of palm wine to God, but now he understood that the daily work of his life should have the same importance.

Such a worldview can enable us to overcome the separation between the sacred and everything else. Our workplace is also God's sphere of influence, God's playing field, and God's interest. In Zaire, God is not just interested in a token splash of palm wine on the ground. God is interested in the use and abuse of palm wine, the health and welfare of the boy who climbed the palm tree, the care and feeding of the chickens, and the nurture and well-being of Mankwela's whole village.

In the United States, God does not limit interest to the offering plates passed around every Sunday morning. God is assuredly more interested in the work, workers, and workplace that provided the wherewithal to have an offering on Sunday mornings. God is holy. That which is offered to God is God's and is holy. The work that yields the offering can be given to God, can be God's work, and can be sacred.

One of the stumbling blocks to appreciating the sacredness of work may be the biblical explanation for the origin of work as we think of it. In Genesis 3 we find the story of The Fall. In brief summary, Adam and Eve were the first humans and lived happily in Paradise, the Garden of Eden. It was a relatively trouble-free life with only one prohibition: They were not to eat from a certain tree. Unfortunately, Adam and Eve were seduced into thinking that God's rules were silly, arbitrary, and oppressive, so they ate from the forbidden tree.

God then pronounced three curses. The serpent would be loathsome and unpopular for the rest of history. The woman would have to endure the pain of childbirth and the arrogance of man. The man would have to work hard in the futile attempt to stay even. In other words, hard work was given as a curse; it was punishment for Adam's participation in the sin against God. If work is punishment and a curse, it is no wonder that we find it hard to think of any work we do as sacred.

I would like to offer other perspectives on the place of work from the creation story in Genesis. First, continuing with Genesis 3 and the curses offered as punishment, remember that childbearing was the curse-punishment given to woman. Yet, today people refer to birth as the greatest miracle; more and more men are joining the birth experience, and more women are opting for natural childbirth. Childbirth may be painful, but it is filled with beauty and wonder. During a Bible study on the subject of the "awesomeness" of God, I asked everyone to think of occasions that filled them with awe, wonder, and the majesty of God. Two people immediately responded with the miracle of birth, bringing new life into the world. One had just married, and the other had just had his third child. Both saw the awesomeness and wonder of God in the very experience that Genesis 3 suggests was given to women as the perpetual reminder of Eve's sin.

I am not arguing that Genesis 3 is all wrong. Still, it seems to be an example of the wisdom that says, "When life gives you the lemons, make lemonade!" There was punishment for Adam and Eve's decision to reject

God's rules, yet God also gives us the ability to repent, be renewed, make the best of every occasion, and make the most from life. The experience of work and birth is complicated and difficult, but God still gives us the right to be redeemed and even to rejoice in the midst of both of these activities.

The Bible tells us of other events and choices that are difficult and even dangerous, but we are still encouraged to pursue them to the glory of God, to turn their very negative aspects into something positive. Death itself is a fact of life, a harsh reality, and the penalty for sin. Despite its inevitability, we are told to live life abundantly with zest, courage, and faith. Jesus said that we are "blessed" when we are reviled and persecuted. We are even challenged to pick up our own cross with all of the obvious ramifications.

The cross is an instrument of torture and execution. Hard work is part of the penalty for rejecting God. Nevertheless, God offers us the chance to take the cross and do the work as centerpieces of our spiritual life. Most people go through life avoiding any contact with any cross and enduring work as a necessary drudgery on the way to the weekend. God offers us the insight that both the cross and work are on the path to eternal life and can be made sacred by dedicating them to God's service.

Work, like the cross, can be tough, but this fact does not take away the possibility of sacredness. Robert Wallace, my successor at First Baptist of Melrose, preached a dynamic sermon titled, "When Peace and Justice Embrace," in which he told about the great South African writer Alan Paton who had some concerns about going to heaven. Paton was sure that God would ask him, "Where are your wounds?" When Paton explained that he had no wounds, God asked, "Was there nothing to fight for?"

When we pick up our cross or go to work, we do so because we know that something is worth doing or fighting for, or that something or someone needs us. The moment we say "yes" to God, what we are doing becomes God's, and it is sacred.

Referring again to the Book of Genesis, we read, "The Lord God took the man and put him in the Garden of Eden to 'work' it and take care of it" (Gen 2:15). In other words, work predated the fall and punishment of Adam and Eve. When Adam lived in Paradise, it must have been lovely, but there was still work to do. Work existed even in Paradise, even while man was still sinless. After Adam and Eve disobeyed God,

God may well have increased the difficulty of work, its urgency, or frustration. Work as a concept and as an activity was an integral part of human life even back when God and Adam were partners in the great adventure of Paradise. Work is not a curse. Work is important to God; it is God-given and sacred.

Genesis 2:15 shows us that work is whatever needs doing. God may have chosen to complicate our lives after the disobedience to God by Adam and Eve, but the reality of "taking care of business" is part of creation; it predated sin and existed in Paradise. Work is whatever comes our way that needs our effort. If we give it our best effort, if it is done in the spirit of a loving God, and if we offer our effort to the glory of God, then it is a theological statement. It is about the Holy; it is sacred.

Endnotes

[1]Traditional, "Sixteen Tons," (New York: Lewis Music Publishing, Co., Inc., 1968).

[2]Studs Terkel, *Working* (New York: Pantheon Books, Random House, 1972).

[3]Ibid., 405.

[4]Ibid., 424.

[5]Ibid., 447-48.

[6]Ibid., xi.

Chapter 3

—The Fire Tender—

I first read about The Fire Tender in the *New York Times*. Every February, for seven years, we took the youth group of our church to New York City to work with the poor and needy in a variety of settings. We set up headquarters at my father's church in Brooklyn, sleeping in the basement, playing in the gym, and interacting with the great diversity of people who make up an exciting urban church. Each day we would tackle some project in an attempt to enhance the lives of poor people. Our young people, ages ten to eighteen, brought love and enthusiasm to every task. They cleaned out abandoned buildings, tore down the decrepit innards of slums, and helped to rebuild. They nailed down floors, scraped and preserved old brick, put up new beams and sheet rock, and painted rooms and hallways.

Over the years, these suburban youngsters became friends with the neighborhood people. They worked together with the families who would eventually move into the resurrected buildings, but they also got to know the poor and homeless people nearby. Across the street from one of our projects lived a gathering of about fifteen people who had taken over an empty lot and built a squatters village. Using big cardboard boxes with all sorts of plastic for insulation, they managed to create their own little neighborhood. Our young people went to visit them, stayed for lunch, became friends, and were invited back. Curiosity turned into friendship, and friendship brought trust. Because of that friendship and trust, the children and homeless people were able to talk together.

The homeless men and women were brutally honest about their lives. They spoke powerfully about their own alcoholism, drug addiction, and personal responsibility for their problems. They spoke about the red tape and bureaucracy that confounded every effort of dignity and self-improvement. They talked about the brutality and inhumanity of the city shelters that forced them to seek refuge in their cardboard community. They also spoke of their love for one another, the compassion and tenderness of people, and their hopes for the future. Above all, they spoke directly to the young people as the ones who have the power to create a world where homelessness, prejudice, and drugs will not ruin lives.

Our young people wanted to do more and know more about the disparately poor people all around them. Each year we tried to add something different to the experience. The most obvious need was for food, so we began to provide groceries for our squatter friends.

A few blocks away was a large park that was heavily populated by homeless people year-round. The park had become a center of controversy and violent confrontation between police, demonstrators, and the homeless people. Despite that history, our young people took delicious, hot dinners that they had cooked at my father's church. Determined to give the personal touch, these teenagers went from one end of the park to the other, from park bench to bandstand to cardboard shanties, delivering dinner.

They delivered much more than dinners, however. They delivered warmth; love; dignity; trust; and a tender, loving touch in a park that frightened the neighborhood and the city—but our experiences helped to overcome the fear. The Bible tells us that "perfect love drives out fear" (1 John 4:18). Every year we saw that promise fulfilled as suburban, naive, young people climbed out of cars and vans "eager to do what is good" (Titus 2:14). Surrounded by filth, crime, poverty, drugs, and every other form of human despair, these children of God were bold in their love and action.

The important thing to know is that this love came from inside each of them. It was real. I did not give them a pep talk that concluded, "Now go out, and be fearless!" Our adult leaders could not order them to be loving. The teenagers did not have to sign a sworn statement promising to be sincere. Instead, all of this goodness came from inside. It had been nurtured by a good Sunday School, a positive youth group, and loving families. So when the kids hit the streets and walked through the horrors of the park, they were able to call upon some inner resources.

As the youngsters approached a homeless person, they exemplified faith at work. They were doing "God stuff." To paraphrase Jesus, they were about their Father's business. They were living out their creed and theology in practical, necessary, urgent, intimate, and direct ways. They were performing "good works," signs of great religion. They took their creed to a dark corner of the park where big men were warming themselves by a fire in a garbage can and drinking from bottles in brown paper bags: "Hi, would you like a hot, home-cooked dinner? We just made it. It's good, I promise!" Then they gave their creed to each man: a piping hot, still fresh, homemade, bountiful dinner.

Others, still children, were also serving their theology. Walking to a park bench, they would gently lift a newspaper off another of God's children to offer food. They would find an old woman walking slowly and fearfully through the park, pushing a shopping cart filled with her whole life-pickings from someone's garbage. She would tense up, afraid of these youngsters, with horrible thoughts running through her mind. Would they mug her, beat her, humiliate her, or kill her? Indeed, homeless people had been murdered and set on fire in the park, but the people who committed such acts of violence were also living out their theology. They were acting out their beliefs; they were serving their lord. Their theology was that of the weapon, hate, and superiority.

Our young people brought their theology wrapped up in an insulated container to keep just right for sharing: "Take, eat, this is my body." No, the kids did not actually say this to the homeless people in the park as Jesus had at the Last Supper. "Here," Jesus was saying, "I have what you need." The theology of these teenagers was just as profound: "Hi, would you like a hot, home-cooked dinner? It's good, I promise!"

One year, as we began to plan the February work camp, I came across the story of The Fire Tender. The Fire Tender was a mysterious, eccentric, middle-aged man who showed up one day on the lower east side of Manhattan and started to cook. He took over an empty lot, gathered some scrap wood, built a fire, put on a kettle and a pot of coffee, and started to peel vegetables. As time went on, the Fire Tender's stew became famous. By the time I visited him, he was feeding a thousand people a day, twenty hours a day. I think he told me it cost him nineteen cents a meal.

The Fire Tender and his wife lived at the empty lot, sleeping in a tent. They were both leftover hippies who had not surrendered their idealism. Yes, they were different. They were not mainstream. They will never be funded. In fact, they had already been forcibly moved from two other empty lots, so we worked with them at their third site.

It amazes me how important an empty lot becomes when some poor people decide to use it. Remember our friends who built a cardboard box community on an empty lot? They actually received an eviction notice! These were disparately poor people who could not receive any city services or benefits because they did not have a legal address. When the "powers that be" wanted to evict them, however, the city knew how to legally contact them!

The situation was likewise with the Fire Tender and his extended family. In this long-forsaken corner of urban hell, where poor people were fed from a stew pot on an empty lot for nineteen cents a meal, suddenly the empty lot became precious property. Subsequently, they were chased from it, but the Fire Tender found another empty lot in that little corner of hell. What a perfect setting for my teenage work-campers from suburban U.S.A.!

While our youngsters cut, peeled, sliced, and diced, I asked the Fire Tender, "Who are all these people. What are they like?" He answered, "Murderers, rapists, drug addicts, pushers, muggers, and the like." I do not know if he was pulling my leg or testing my resolve. They sure looked like what we expect such people to look like, but as they lined up for their stew, bantered back and forth with the kids, and helped wash the pans at the fire hydrant, they seemed just like people—neighbors, even friends. There comments were varied:

> "You a Baptist? I'm a Baptist!"
> "Hey, you with the Yankee hat, I'm a Met fan. You must be crazy!"
> "Hey, sweet thing, what are you doing here? This is your vacation? You *paid* to come here? You are crazy. God bless you. We love you."

Late one afternoon, before the evening winter cold set in and the dinner rush began, I sat down with the Fire Tender in the tent. I felt it was time for me to learn something profound, deep, and spiritual. I wanted to learn this truth from someone who lived and worked on the cutting edge of real ministry. I asked him, "Why do you do this?" He looked at me with incredible patience and answered, "Isn't it obvious." It was a statement, not a question. It was a creed and a theology.

Faith at work is a theology of the obvious. Years ago, the comedian, Flip Wilson had a popular television show. One of his weekly skits had him portraying a minister: the pastor of "The Church of What's Happening Now." Everyone thought it was funny, outrageous, and a bit irreverent.

The Fire Tender lived in the world of the obvious. So, on one corner of the world of the obvious, he established a "church of what's happening now." This church ministered to people who were hungry, lonely, thirsty, hopeless, and cold. For the Fire Tender, the solution to their problems was single, cheap, and obvious. He took over an empty lot, gathered some fire wood, put on a stew pot and kettle of coffee, and invited the neighbors—a thousand of them. He was simply following the example in Luke 14:

> Someone gave a great dinner and invited many. At the time for the dinner, he sent his slave to say to those who had been invited, "Come, for everything is ready now." (vv. 16-17)

In this story, the man hosting the banquet expected it to be a wonderful affair with good food, good friends, and good times. Something went wrong. Everyone who was expected to attend made excuses and chose not to attend. They had business reasons, family responsibilities, or financial considerations. As each potential guest considered the banquet, he or she decided it was not important or necessary—a low priority. The invited guests had better things to do with their time and other people they preferred. The master of the dinner would not let the food, the evening, or the joy go to waste, however. He wanted the banquet hall filled with people who wanted and needed to be there.

So the servants were sent into the back streets, alleys, and forgotten corners of the countryside, among the lonely and outcasts to issue invitations to any and all persons who would come. The poor, sick, homeless, unwanted, unwashed, unpopular, disliked, wretched, and suffering people were brought to fill the seats at the great dinner.

My friend, the Fire Tender, was such a servant. In his world of the obvious, he looked around at his neighbors and saw urgent and appalling need. Society, too busy with priorities, could not imagine needing what the Fire Tender offered at his corner lot great dinner. Most people could not imagine wanting to be surrounded by the riffraff of the neighborhood, but the Fire Tender saw them as guests, friends, and neighbors.

Mahatma Gandhi also lived in a society where a large portion of the population was considered unwanted, unpopular, unclean, and "untouchable." But Gandhi called the untouchables "harijans," children of God.[1]

In the world of the obvious, through the "church of what's happening now," our task is to see people as God sees them and love them as God loves us. The world of the obvious needs to be governed by a theology of the obvious. Discussion of issues such as the trinity, transubstantiation, and eschatology may be important, interesting matters of faith, but they are not obvious.

The world of the obvious requires a theology of the obvious. Faith at work seeks to be obvious theology. It says that in a city where thousands are hungry, we should take an empty lot, gather firewood, tap water from the fire hydrant, and boil it in a big kettle, toss in donated vegetables, and meet and feed the hungry.

I have not met Mother Teresa, but I have seen her work in Calcutta, which is a direct response to the biblical principles of work. Abandoned children are taken in, loved, and nurtured. Dying people found on street corners and in alley ways are tenderly touched and caressed, living out their final days in dignity. I am sure there is a time and place for spirited debate about the difference between Hinduism's reincarnation and Christianity's judgment day, but Mother Teresa's home for the dying is not it. When my family visited there, I was drawn to a young German man in the corner who was cradling a young Indian in his arms. Softly and gently he stroked the man's hand, whispering assurances of love and nearness. This was faith at work at its best, a Christian doing what was most needed in a way that was thoroughly pure and loving.

No book has touched my life more than Dominique Lappierre's *City of Joy*.[2] It tells the dramatic story of the squatter settlements in Calcutta and the daily heroism of the world's poorest people. Father Stephen Kovalski, a young Polish priest, chose to live and minister in the slum. Theologically trained, Father Kovalski could easily have out-argued and verbally bedazzled the Moslems and Hindus who lived there. With the entire population in a daily struggle to survive, the whole community lived at death's door.

What better time and place to bring to bear the weight of such theological subjects as sin, death, repentance, atonement, and hell? But a boy, dying in excruciating pain, needed morphine. A dying rickshaw puller wanted to see his daughter properly married before surrendering his cadaver to the skeleton brokers. The lepers were too feeble to escape the rising flood waters. There was the local mafia chieftain's heart to soften.

Father Kovalski saw need everywhere. It was all obvious. The God of love was constantly calling for those who would "do all that I commanded" (Matt 28:20), who would fulfill the commandments ("the greatest of these is love," [1 Cor 13]), who would love their neighbor and enemy, and who would do unto the least of these as if they were doing it directly for Jesus. Simply stated, the theology of the obvious became more urgent than the theology of leisure and academia—not better or more true, just more urgent.

Jesus was the master of the obvious. His three-year ministry was a constant response to the needs and opportunities placed immediately before him. He rarely had to go out of his way to meet an opportunity waiting to be grabbed, a need waiting to be met, or a person waiting to be loved.

When Jesus fed the multitude of over 5,000, he did not require a Ph.D. to see the need. The crowd sat before him, listening, all day long. He took what was offered—a few loaves of bread and fish—gave thanks, blessed the food, and shared it. When ten leprous outcasts cried "Lord, have mercy," the miracle-in-waiting was all set. When the friends of a paralytic on a cot lowered him from the roof above, everything that Jesus needed was available. When the woman who was troubled by endless bleeding pushed through the crowd to touch the hem of Jesus' robe, he felt the touch and, more importantly, felt the need. The disciples wondered how Jesus could distinguish any one touch, but for Jesus it was obvious.

A face, a look, a touch, a cry, an act, a word—these captured Jesus' attention. These incidents were nothing spectacular—just obvious, everyday occurrences that Jesus noticed. There was no shout from heaven saying, "Heal the lepers," or archangel pointing out the woman who was bleeding; or divine handwriting on the wall telling Jesus to notice the paralytic.

Jesus lived in the world of the obvious. He did whatever needed doing as it came his way. Without publicity, hype, or fanfare; without concern for safety, decorum, or what others would think; without hesitation, a federally-funded study, or legislation—Jesus just did it. Nike may own the trademark to the slogan "Just Do It," and Bo Jackson may have popularized it, but Jesus lived it.

The Fire Tender was the person who simplified my search for an adequate theology capable of defining a social activism. "It's obvious," he said. Father Kovalski's witness in *The City of Joy* gives me the dose of inspiration we all need to keep motivated toward caring. Jesus gives us the right to call this obvious stuff of work a real theology, genuine God-talk, and a spiritual construct on which we can hang our determination to love fully, personally, and directly. Jesus, the carpenter from Nazareth, raises the tools of our doing to the level of instruments of worship.

Endnotes

[1]M. K. Gandhi, *Non-Violent Resistance* (New York: Schocken Books, 1961) vii.

[2]Dominique Lappierre, *City of God* (Garden City NY: Doubleday & Co., 1985).

Chapter 4

—The Example of Jesus—

Jesus exalted work by doing work himself, just as Jesus exalted humanity by being human. Tradition relates that Jesus was a carpenter, learning the trade from his earthly father. He could make, build, construct, pound, cut, and earn a living. The least exotic but most plausible explanation of "the missing years" of Jesus life—from ages twelve to thirty—is that he did his apprenticeship as a carpenter, learned the craft, practiced it, and supported the family with it. If so, Jesus knew all about callouses, slivers, cuts, budgets, purchasing, pricing, inflation, and all of the other everyday concerns of the working person. Jesus worked.

When Jesus began a public ministry at age thirty, he again made a conscious decision to work. He did not have to. According to Matthew 4:1-11, when Jesus was confronted by Satan in the wilderness, he was given every opportunity and excuse to take the easy way out. Satan pointed out that Jesus did not have to worry about putting food on the table, the usual excuse for working: "Just snap your fingers, and turn the stones into bread. You don't need to work to get what you need."

Even more attractive was Satan's final offer: "Let's make a deal out here in the privacy of the wilderness, with nobody watching; bow down and worship me. I'll give you the world on a silver patter!" In other words, "You don't need to work to get what you want."

Why do I call it an attractive offer? Remember, Jesus' calling—his vocation and job—was to be the Messiah. That was his work. His job description was to save the world. Suddenly, Satan was taking away the two main reasons for going to work: to put food on the table (earn a living, pay the bills) and to accomplish a given task. Satan offered to do the work for Jesus and reminded him that his every personal need could be met without any effort.

Satan's approach was not Jesus' style, however. Jesus commanded Satan to go away. In effect, he said, "I've got work to do. Don't tempt me with some easy way out. I'm proud of my work. I'll do my work. I don't need excuses." Jesus made a conscious decision. In Christ, God has chosen to become fully human, and part of the human condition is that we get what we work for and reap what we sow; there is no free lunch.

So Jesus got down to work. He chose work. For the next three years, he worked at his craft as skillfully and diligently as he had done in the carpenter's shop. In spiritual terms, Jesus continued to pound, cut, make, build, and construct, but this time his project was the kingdom of God rather than a cradle or a table. The Gospel show us that Jesus was a precise, diligent, tireless, and reliable worker. He took obvious pride in his work; he did it with integrity. Furthermore, Jesus was keen to share what he knew, willing to get his hands dirty, and perfectly willing to delegate. Jesus was, in every way, a worker worth studying and emulating.

In the last twenty years, there have been several popular renditions of the life of Jesus. On Broadway, we saw *Jesus Christ, Superstar* and *Godspell.* I remember *Jesus Christ, Superstar* as dark and brooding, hinting at powerful and conflicting forces even within Jesus. *Godspell* was filled with youthful enthusiasm and joy, fast and fun. Off-Broadway brought *The Cotton Patch Gospel,* a blue-grass, countrified musical based on Clarence Jordan's popular retelling of the Jesus story in a southern context. A national tour featured the renowned Shakespearean actor Alec McGowen simply but dynamically reading *The Gospel of Mark.* Other outstanding productions were the Academy Award winning movie *The Gospel According to Saint Matthew* and the controversial *The Last Temptation of Christ.*

Personally, I like all of these shows. I find myself agreeing with Paul (Phil 1:14-18), who sat in prison hearing all sorts of cellmates talking about Christ. Some of them mocked, while others questioned or doubted. Paul was happy with anything that kept Jesus in the forefront, however, for every question, joke, or comment was an opportunity to tell the fuller and loving story of Christ.

I remember when *The Last Temptation of Christ* opened in Boston. Protesters, marchers, and placards greeted us as we lined up for tickets. Police searched us as we entered the theater. I wondered if the popcorn was poisoned! On the screen I saw something profound that resonated with the two other theatrical presentations that had moved me the most, McGowen's reading of *Mark* and Pasolini's film on *Matthew.* All of these portrayed a hard-working Jesus Christ.

I had one overwhelming impression from Pasolini's *Matthew*: Jesus was in a hurry. Whatever he was doing was important and urgent. I remember Jesus rushing about and the disciples hustling to catch up. Every moment was precious; there was no time to waste.

In *The Last Temptation of Christ*, I was moved by a Jesus who could sweat and be dirty. The film gave the impression that being the Messiah was hard work. The very act of saving the world by first dying for the sins of the world was an arduous, painful, demanding, and exhausting task. To paraphrase an old advertisement, Jesus saved the world the old-fashioned way; he earned it. By the sweat of his brow, the breaking of his body, the offering of his time, the use of his gifts, and the sharing of the essence of his life, Jesus did his job.

The most lasting image of Jesus for me was McGowen's reading of *Mark*. McGowen entered the small theater, placed a small Bible on a table on the bare stage, and for the next two hours captivated the audience with his reading of the Old English King James Version. There were no props, theatrics, nor sound track—just the word. Then, just at the point where Jesus told the disciples what they were to do, McGowen added the only dramatic flourish of the evening. He rolled up his sleeves and told them that they would get dirty, would likely sweat, and may work quickly and hard, but the work was important.

Faith at work makes the same points. Work is important. It has nothing to do with income level, prestige, or some jobs being more valued than others. The idea of faith at work is not comparative or competitive and does not seek to say that one person's work is better than another's, or more important, or more spiritual. One's theology of work is entirely personal. It asks me to think about what I am doing, how every effort of my life can be sacred if I offer it to God, and how the energy I use can make a difference through serving God. It does not allow room for arrogance, smugness, spiritual conceit, or any other "holier-than-thou" attitudes. Faith at work simply says: There is God-given work to do, and every one of us has God-given talents and opportunities to do some of it.

Look specifically at how Jesus conducted his work. First and foremost, it seems that Jesus broke all the rules. He did not care if his work was on a weekday or the weekend, for the rich or poor, with a friend or an enemy, at home or on the road or in foreign territory, in private or in public, or open to criticism or praise. He took every opportunity to do his work.

Jesus set this tone with his first miracle. At a wedding in Cana (John 2:1-11), the reception party ran out of wine. Truthfully, Jesus seemed perturbed to be bothered by such a trifle. Jesus asked his mother why she involved him. Nevertheless, something needed to be done. Jesus was in a position to do it and had the ability. He turned water into wine, thereby saving the day. In the scheme of things, it was a small miracle done in an unimportant setting. How many people in the modern church might wonder if this miracle was an appropriate use of divine power? With a world to be saved from sin, death to be conquered, and the kingdom of God to be established, why give wedding guests an extra glass of wine?

Yet Jesus did turn the water into wine. He was willing to be a party to a fun and festive occasion. If his gifts could help a wedding celebration continue, help the host family avoid embarrassment, and respond to the gentle request of his mother, so be it. Jesus' first miracle was not world-changing, earth-shattering, or soul-saving; but it was special to the group of people in Cana.

This story was just the beginning of an unlikely ministry that was carried out in unlikely ways among unlikely people. While opposing the religious leadership of the day, Jesus met with the Pharisee Nicodemus to discuss spiritual matters (John 3). He traveled into the land of the outcasts, Samaria, bringing "living water" (John 4:10) to a woman and a people of questionable reputation. Soon, Jesus was spending time with publicans and sinners, attracting the scorn of "better people." He touched society's untouchables, loved the unloveables, and forgave the adulterous woman caught red-handed. Jesus seemed to have no sense of propriety, boundaries, limits, or community standards. If a job needed doing, and he was there to do it, he did it.

Matthew 12 contains two telling stories about Jesus' approach to work. The chapter begins with Jesus and the disciples walking through a grain field on the Sabbath. Because they were hungry, they picked some grains and popped them into their mouths—a sort of mindless snack during a leisurely walk. The Pharisees saw this activity as a violation of one of the countless laws governing what a person could and could not do on the Sabbath, however. Work was absolutely out of the question on the Sabbath, and the harvesting of grains was a clear violation. Jesus turned the whole legalistic world upside down, though. As Jesus said in Mark 2:27, "The Sabbath was made for man, not man for the Sabbath."

As if to drive home the point, Jesus went immediately to a synagogue and healed a man with a crippled hand (Matt 12; Mark 3). Although people could quibble about whether plucking a few grains for a snack really constituted work, the overt act of using one's powers and gifts to heal another person was clearly work. Even Jesus recognized it as work, but it was something that should be done, and he could do it, so he did it. He could have waited until the next day, returned another time, or sent the man to other people and places with reputations for healing. Jesus did not conduct his work in such a way, however. Opportunity, faith, and will all came together and produced a miracle. Jesus would not allow anything to get in the way of doing the work God gave him to do.

Also, Jesus did what he could. He met the opportunities that came his way with the full force of his love directed to each unique opportunity. He did not try to conquer the Roman Empire, and he refused Satan's inference that he wave a magic wand and win the world in one fell swoop, but Jesus faced the everyday challenges with confidence and intensity.

The athlete knows that the key to a great athletic performance is to "stay within oneself." The great runner does not lunge, but runs smoothly and consistently. The great pitcher does not overthrow. The great hitter does not swing too hard. The great manager does not overmanage. Instead, we are encouraged to do well at what we can do, just as Jesus did.

Jesus kept his eyes open for the chance to serve. He did not end the woman's monthly cycle, but healed the woman whose hemorrhaging was out of control. He did not destroy famine, but fed the 5,000 people sitting in front of him. He did not return humanity to the immortality of paradise by doing away with death, but offered us a path through death if we so choose. He did not end the sin of prejudice, but healed the lepers and made the Samaritan the unlikely hero of the great parable. He did not do away with the criminal justice system, but promised paradise to the one thief on the cross whose heart was open to change. He did not end the tyranny of oppressive taxes, but turned Zacchaeus into an honest man. He did not eliminate disease from the earth, but risked criticism to heal a handicapped person on the Sabbath. He did not wipe out religious tyranny, but poked fun at it. Jesus simply did what he could—without debate, hesitation, or second thoughts.

The principle of faith at work implies that some things are obvious and do not require any debate. Whether the clergy actually turn the bread and wine into the literal blood and body of Jesus may be worthy of debate. Issues such as the practical application of the gifts of the Spirit today, whether or not the mother Mary was forever a virgin, the benefits of intercessory prayer, and whether or not Peter walked on the water can all be interesting fodder for Bible studies and classrooms.

Outside the classroom where life is mostly lived, however, the things that need doing are rather clear. As the Fire Tender said, some things are obvious. We do not need, indeed we should not allow ourselves, to debate whether or not to feed the hungry, clothe the naked, or visit the lonely. Some things cry out for our attention, action, and love. Some things are so obvious and urgent that it may well be blasphemous to waste any time in discussion.

Years ago, I read a book that was written by a missionary in Africa. He told of getting behind in his official work. One night, he decided to stay up late to work on all the official reports and denominational paperwork piling up on his desk. He was focused and determined to get it done. A persistent knocking on the door of his mission house did not interrupt him; he ignored it. The knocking continued from time to time, but was not very loud. Soon it stopped completely, and the missionary was successful in completing the top priority paperwork for his denomination, some of which was quite urgent. The next morning, the missionary opened his front door. A dead man lay at the foot of the door. His last, desperate hope had been to crawl to the mission house. Inside, the missionary had been too busy doing his work.

"I am standing at the door, knocking," said Jesus (Rev 3:20). He also said that the stranger at the door desperately seeking out care, daring to believe that we will care, is the very Lord we try so earnestly to worship. Whenever we do or fail to do for the least person, it is the same as loving or failing to love our savior.

Tom Hall, a long-time friend and colleague, told the story of a mangy, little, yellow bird who became convinced that the sky was falling. The sorry little bird tried to warn everyone else, but no one would listen. Finally, the creature took matters into its own hands. As people went about their business, they noticed the tiny, yellow bird, lying on its back, with its spindly little legs straight up in the air, struggling with all of its might to hold up the sky. Friends and strangers came to laugh, watch, and ridicule, but the bird knew what it was doing. When the mocking onlookers asked the purpose of this silly spectacle, the yellow bird answered confidently, "One does what one can." Not much more or much less is asked of us. We are given the privilege of doing what we can.

Perhaps the greatest quality in Jesus' work was the grace with which he approached his work and co-workers. Jesus was always one to look into the heart of the matter to see the spirit, attitude, and emotion within each encounter. He could sense the concern in the Roman centurion's heart for his servant, so Jesus healed the servant. The sorrow surrounding Lazarus' death caused Jesus to weep, so he raised Lazarus from the dead. The woman with the hemorrhage touched Jesus so profoundly that he "felt virtue" flow out of him, and she was healed. He could look into the eyes of Peter, Zacchaeus, and Thomas and read the remorse in their souls, so each of them was given a fresh start. Jesus did not look for perfection. He was satisfied to find earnestness, sincerity, and determination.

I remember the first time I was in school where a teacher gave two grades in each course. The numerical grade reflected test results. The letter grade measured effort. Suddenly, I felt a great burden lifted from my shoulders. I felt liberated from the results-oriented, bottom-line philosophy of education. The new grading system allowed me the chance to get a seventy-five in math class with an A- in effort. It was the teacher's way of saying, "Listen, kid, you're not very coordinated when it comes to math, but at least you're trying." A seventy-five no longer meant that a student was automatically bad, or did not try, or did not care.

This grading system also allowed teachers to send other messages. It meant I could get a ninety-two in English class with a C in effort, which said to me, "Kid, you're sliding by, and I know it. You love to read and write, so you're doing better than most, but you haven't even begun to tap your potential. Why don't you try to find out what you are really capable of doing?"

A seventy-five in math class with a C effort also sent a powerful message: "You're not doing well, and you're not even trying, so we have no idea what you're made of in this class. We don't know what you can do, and you're not giving any of us—including yourself—a chance to find out."

Occasionally, I would get the best message of all: good test grades with a solid mark in effort. I was doing well and giving my best. I liked the new grading system. From then on attitude, effort, and spirit counted.

Jesus teaches us the same lesson about work. He grades us on our attitude, our effort, and the spirit we bring to our work. Spirit counts. We live in an age that worships the bottom line. We are numbers-oriented and statistics-driven. Results are only measured by whether what we do has become bigger, greater, longer, more popular, more profitable, and more famous. In the world of the obvious, however, where Jesus invites us to pick up a tool along with our cross, spirit counts.

Robert Schuller has the right emphasis in his book about the Beatitudes, *The Be-happy Attitudes*. The Beatitudes are about attitudes. Jesus was intensely interested in what was going on inside the hearts, minds, and spirits of persons. In the two great commandments (Mark 12:28-31), he begged us to be thoroughly immersed in love, inside and out. Likewise, love must be at the heart of faith at work.

Even though the biblical principle of work is a call to Christian people to do what needs doing, God is far more interested in how and why we do than how much we do. The issue is never the number of people we served, but how many people we served humbly. On judgment day, the question will not be how many people we helped, but how many we helped lovingly. When people talk about "good works," the emphasis is too often on the "works" and not on the "good." We should not lose sight of this adjective, however. The word "works" is a noun, entirely neutral in morality. Nothing is inherently positive, effective, or godly about "works." Work may be filled with potential, but we determine what to make of that potential and what will become of the "works." Many adjectives can appear in front of "works": bad, useless, futile, wasted, and so on. But our attitude as well as our effort can result in "good" works.

All forms of Christian ministry face the challenge of maintaining the proper attitude so that we may produce good works. How do we keep alive the original version of the Gospel, the same spirit of Christ, the everlasting commitment to live the life of Jesus? All too easily we become slaves to property, bottom-line budgets, status quo, being well thought of, and/or survival.

I correspond with Stephen Jones, pastor of the Central Baptist Church in Wayne, Pennsylvania. His church letterhead declares the church to be "a caring and risking community of faith"—the perfect blend of "good" and "works." If this church succeeds even partially in being a caring and risking community of faith, then the members are living their faith at work. Their caring is the attitude part; their risking is the work part. Doing work with the proper attitude as a community of faith produces a living theology.

Jesus was a firm advocate for the primacy of attitude, effort, and spirit. He called people to courage, sacrifice, and compassion. As I have said to thousands of people in sermons and Bible studies, "God does not ask us to be successful, just obedient."

In Mark 14, we find Jesus visiting a home in Bethany. Unexpectedly, a women anointed Jesus with very expensive perfume. Just as unexpectedly, she was rebuked by some of the "holier-than-thou" folks in the house who tried to shame her for the wastefulness. Jesus was not counting dollars and cents or gauging the bottom line, however. Jesus preferred to understand the heart of the woman. What was she doing? What was her spirit? Why this effort? What was this work?

Then Jesus offered four interesting thoughts, three of which are still mostly ignored. The one that everyone remembers is "The poor you will always have with you" (Mark 14:7), which some Christians have used as an excuse for not doing anything about poverty. In reality, Jesus was stating the obvious that was about to become painfully obvious: Jesus' time on earth was soon to come to a violent end, so the time to minister to him directly and personally was almost over. Therefore, the woman should be allowed the extravagance of showing her love. The other three thoughts, mostly forgotten statements, deserve attention. Jesus said,

> She has done a beautiful thing to me. . . . She has done what she could.
> . . . Wherever the gospel is preached in the whole world, what she has done will be told. (Mark 14:6-9 RSV)

The woman's deed was beautiful to Jesus and deserves to be told in concert with the Gospel: Her attitude and spirit beautified the effort of faith at work. Dare I say that the work itself may very well have been secondary?

When I was crisscrossing the world on behalf of Habitat for Humanity, I often told people that when the history of the organization is written we might discover that the actual, physical house is only the fourth or fifth most important product of the ministry. More important may be the breaking down of walls and barriers that separate humanity into warring factions of race, tribe, gender, religion, caste, and class. When an older man affirms the carpentry skills of a young woman, a high-caste Brahmin builds a house for an untouchable, Christians and Muslims work together, affluent college students use spring break to live and work with the poor, and blacks and whites stand together—"they have done a beautiful thing," in addition to doing what they could. Faith at work cries out for a beautiful spirit in concert with effective work.

Jesus carried out his work with integrity. He never took advantage of people, exploited or used people, or deceived people. There is a fine line between being focused and being obsessed, and Jesus never crossed that line. He was never interested in proving his manhood. He was not surly in apparent defeat nor arrogant in certain victory. His path was not littered with people he had tossed aside, stepped over, or crossed. If anything, Jesus set the example of going the extra mile, even with people who disappointed him.

The disciples were often slow learners, but he stuck with them. They argued about who would have the best seats in heaven. Peter denied him three times. The two men he found walking toward Emmaus had given up on him. Thomas would not believe the Resurrection until he could see and touch the wounds in Jesus' body. These were the responses of the people Jesus knew best and with whom he had worked the hardest, but he never gave up on anyone. His sense of integrity was such that once he had made a commitment to a person and formed a relationship, there was a bond forever.

When Paul defined love in 1 Corinthians 13, one of the most amazing attributes he listed was that "love never ends." This is a tough definition to accept and a difficult standard to uphold. Jesus spoke a lot about love, offering love as the cornerstone of the fresh message we call the Good News. Never-ending love—which is patient, kind, and self-sacrificing—was the basis for Jesus' integrity. Because he was such a loving person, he was unable to turn away from someone in need, give up on someone who was a disappointment, or quit on someone who failed him. Jesus was incapable of being unforgiving or unloving.

In Hebrews 13:8, it is written, "Jesus Christ is the same yesterday and today and forever." This verse symbolizes my personal definition of integrity: consistency, reliability, and dependability. A person with integrity is someone who has certain threads woven throughout his/her whole being, and those threads hold the person together no matter what the circumstance, pressure, or temptation. Jesus was such a person of integrity. Yesterday, today, or tomorrow; in the company of the rich or the poor, the powerful or the weak; and in public or private, Jesus could be counted on to be the same.

Furthermore, Jesus was truthful in the performance of his work and his promises to those who would join the work. They were offered the chance to be "fishers of men" (Matt 4:19), but they were also promised persecution, no place to lay their head, strife, and a cross. Jesus held nothing back.

I spoke with a great leader in Christian mission about a job. He wanted me to join the staff, was uncertain about my assignment, and wanted me to replace a long-time partner (whom we would not tell of the plans). Duties were abstract, and the salary was vague. Other than that, everything was on the up and up! The sad thing is that the job is a good work done with good people. It has the potential to be something great, but I believe the organization is held back by the lack of a thorough, all-encompassing integrity.

Christ's work requires a standard of integrity from the top to the bottom, in issues large or small, when dealing with petty cash or millions, in private meetings or public pronouncements, and in personal morality and corporate decisions. When we fall short, we must confess, repent, change, and recommit to integrity.

Lack of integrity weakens work anywhere. Work suffers when ethics, words, and/or behavior change from yesterday to today to tomorrow—depending on the setting, who is watching, or what can be gotten away with. Jesus set a high standard for integrity at work, but it is not impossibly high.

Jesus stayed focused. He never lost sight of the purpose of his work. Because he served in the public arena, certainly he had many opportunities to be drawn away from his focus. He was befriended and respected by the rich and powerful. Nicodemus, a Pharisee, sought Jesus' help and was profoundly grateful. Matthew and Zacchaeus had served the Roman government in official capacities as tax collectors. Jesus dined with others in that political circle. A wealthy man, Joseph of Arimathea, received permission to bury Jesus, so they likely had a relationship. Jesus had gained a good deal of popularity in the countryside and was given a hero's welcome when he entered Jerusalem on Palm Sunday. Later, Pontius Pilate seemed anxious to find some way to release Jesus.

Jesus could easily have nurtured those relationships into profitable, productive alliances. With his charisma and spiritual gifts combined with political and religious clout, he could have become a formidable force. A little "schmoozing" here and there, being seen with the right people, a few celebrity endorsements, a willingness to play along and turn the other way when necessary, more flexibility in his lifestyle, a less stringent code of ethics, a careful stroking of the right people with the right connections—such openness could have given him a long life, a great career, and a huge following. Who knows how much good Jesus could have accomplished if he had not been so narrowly focused!

This idea is the popular rationale for all of the popular leaders who lose their way and tumble into scandal. Whether it is a hunger for young women or boys, extravagant lifestyle or power, celebrity status or popular acclaim, these people misstep. Their followers or fans prop them up, however, telling themselves, "But we need them, they speak so good, they raise money, they help the poor, they save souls, they do good, and so on."

Maybe this is the reason why Jesus did not live very long, but his job was not to live long. Instead, his job consisted of a lot of actions and statements that would lead to an early death. He knew the cost, the odds, and the outcome, and he knew his job. Because Jesus stayed focused and was not seduced by side benefits, the entire human family has the gift of eternal life available.

Jesus invited everyone to share in his work. He saw in it the opportunity for a community response. After his baptism and the temptations in the wilderness, the first thing Jesus did was to develop a community of co-workers. Long before American management and pastoral leadership theory talked about empowerment and enabling, Jesus was living those concepts.

The disciples were given power to do "greater things" than Jesus did (John 14:12). He set an example for them, taught them, trained them, and set them free to do their work. They were sent out two by two to test their abilities (Mark 6:6-13), then brought back for fine-tuning; and then the great work of Jesus' life was turned over to them.

Jesus held nothing back from his co-workers and colleagues. He told them that they were not to think of themselves in any diminished way; they were to have the self-confidence and affirmation that comes with being friends (John 15:14, 15). Finally, in their last moments together, Jesus delivered the job description, the Great Commission, into their hands:

Go therefore and make disciples of all nations, baptizing them in the name of the Father and of the Son and of the Holy Spirit, and teaching them to obey everything I have commanded you. (Matt 28:19, 20)

Jesus entrusted the great work of his life to those who chose to work with him. He dared to believe that they, we, could make a significant contribution to his work. He was even willing to risk our failures, shortcomings, mistakes, and foolishness. Unlikely as it seems, Jesus is like the master painter who invites all of us to take a brush and help to paint the greatest painting of all time.

Unfortunately, our churches, religious institutions, and corporations are often headed by megalomaniacs whose egos permit them only to count on themselves. More than selfish, they ascribe to themselves a level of divinity rejected even by God. They imagine that everything rides on their own shoulders. In times of success, they are self-centered: "I, I, I . . . I do this, I decide that." In times of failure, however, they place blame elsewhere: "They . . . they did this, they did that."

Interestingly enough, for all of the omnipotence, omniscience, and omnipresence of God, God never minds sharing the stage. In the act of creation, God, operating as Trinity, spoke in the plural: "Let us make humankind in our own image" (Gen 1:26). Thousands of years later, the very son of God invited us to join in the new creation as friends, co-workers, and partners in the vineyard—partners in the great enterprise of saving the world and building the kingdom of God.

Ultimately, in the doing of our work, we become family. Paul wrote in Romans 8:14, 16, 17:

All who who are led by the Spirit of God are children of God. . . . It is the very Spirit bearing witness . . . that we are children of God, and if children, then heirs, heirs of God and joint heirs with Christ—in fact, we suffer with him so that we may be glorified with him.

While the whole world tries to figure out how to revitalize industry and stem the tide of recession, and while Christian ministries revert to top-down management style and closed systems, Jesus invites us to share in the world—the sufferings and the glory—with the promise to be full partners, co-heirs, and joint-venturers.

I am particularly in awe of Jesus' own spiritual life in the midst of his work. We think we are "spiritual" when we do good, act overtly

Christian, or engage in some specific ministry. I am drawn to the occasion when, at the point of exhaustion and after conducting ministry, Jesus broke away to work on his own spirituality.

Chapter six of Mark's Gospel reports an especially tiring time in Jesus' life. Jesus' popularity was at its height, and more than 5,000 people gathered so that he could teach them. Already exhausted, the day certainly drained Jesus even more. At the conclusion of the day, after the crowd had miraculously been fed with just five loaves of bread and two fish, Jesus

> immediately made his disciples get into the boat and go on ahead . . . to Bethsaida, while he dismissed the crowd. After saying farewell to them, he went up on a mountainside to pray (vv. 45, 46).

This extraordinary event tells us more about Jesus than we may realize at first. Most of Jesus' miracles are outside of our experience. Walking on water, healing a handicapped person, raising Lazarus from the dead, and cleansing the lepers are beyond anything we can imagine. When Jesus went to the mountainside to pray, however, he accomplished a miracle that we need and can enjoy.

We have all been exhausted and drained, with nothing more to offer, no more effort to give, and no more energy or ideas or will. We have reached wit's end; we have been burned out, used up, and emptied. At the workplace, in our personal lives, on the athletic field, at school, and in relationships, we have gone to the well once too often and found it dry. We need a miracle, therapy, or some remedy. Do not overlook Jesus' approach to work. When we have done all we can and yet there is more to do, why not go to the mountainside and pray?

We have no idea of what we are capable of doing. We barely touch the surface of our capabilities. I once heard that before we die, we should make sure that we are all used up. In sports, I have always told my daughter and son and the teams I have coached to leave everything out on the field and have absolutely nothing left over. Most of the time, though, we do not know how to dig deeper and come up with more to give.

People think it is New Age heresy to talk about "getting centered," but, according to Luke 5:16, Jesus made it a habit. Jesus often withdrew to lonely places and prayed, as opposed to the modern practices of taking stimulant drugs or no longer caring or doing. He chose to get in touch with the God who is the source of all energy, the giver of all tasks, and the provider of all opportunities.

I do not suggest using a renewed spiritual life in place of rest or a vacation, but committed Christians should stop using rest or vacation in place of a renewed spiritual life. We should not assume we hold the solution to our problems. More often than not, we need to get to the mountainside or lonely places to get centered through prayer with the God of all work. We always assume the problem is us, so the solution must be in us. The idea that the solution is beyond us, waiting at the mountainside, does not sit well with our theories. We are too self-centered in our problems and our solutions.

God does give us work to do and is a tough task master, demanding, with high standards. Yet, God does not expect us to do our work alone, have a breakdown, suffer burn-out, or quit. Like an enlightened boss, it is in God's best interest to keep us going, happy, and healthy. We can do the work by paying attention to our spiritual lives, realizing that we are not and should not be alone, reminding ourselves that "two or three gathered together" is more effective, visiting the mountainside, and opening up to the presence and power of God's continued Spirit. (By the way, Jesus went to the mountainside exhausted, drained, and seemingly empty of all that he could give. After praying on the mountainside, he walked on the water.)

With Jesus, there is always work to do. The most lamentable (and maybe we just need the first four letters of that word, l-a-m-e!) excuse in all the earth is, "There's nothing I can do. I can't make a difference; it's useless." Such talk will not impress the Christ who tells us, "For God all things are possible" (Matt 19:26). We are not given permission to do nothing. Years ago, I saw a cartoon in which the two characters noticed a third character dangling over the edge of a cliff, hanging just by the fingertips. One turned to the other and said, "The government oughta do something!" Wrong—somebody should reach out a hand or call 911. Do something!

The spring of 1992 was filled with ugly troubling images, captured on videotape and often shown live on television. We watched the police beating of Rodney King, the rioting and looting of Los Angeles, the merciless beating of a truck driver, and the torching of businesses. There were other images if we cared to notice. One family, watching the beating of the truck driver shown live on their living room T.V., rushed immediately to the scene and saved the man's life. A black minister saw a Mexican carpenter about to be murdered. He intervened, sheltered the Mexican with his own body, and called for help. Others left the safety of their homes to go into the devastated areas with brooms and shovels to begin the cleanup even before the destruction ended. Life is not always such a dramatic crisis. We are not always called to be courageous or heroic. Sometimes only the little things in life call out to us.

We think of Jesus as the Messiah, the Son of God, the one who died on the cross, the savior of the world. We remember him cleansing the Temple, raising the dead, and standing stoic before Pilate. Jesus' life was not all spectacular, front-page stuff, however. He blessed the little children, looked up into a tree to find Zacchaeus, sought out the two disconsolate men walking to Emmaus, and affirmed Martha and Mary. In his parables and in his life, he treasured the lost coin, the lost sheep, and the least of any category we care to mention. Nothing was too small or insignificant to be done.

Our days are filled with some things that need doing. It is the doing of nothing that is unacceptable. The parable of the talents (Matt 25:14-28) offers the same principle of work. In the parable, Jesus told of a man who had to go away and left three servants in charge of his business. They were given varying degrees of responsibility, described as talents. The servant who was given five talents and the servant who was given two talents both used what they had to the best of their ability and were successful. When the master heard an accounting from those two servants, his response was the same:

> Well done, good and trustworthy slave; you have been trustworthy in a few things; I will put you in charge of many things; enter into the joy of your master. (v. 21)

The third servant, unfortunately, squandered his opportunity. Frozen by fear, he chose the easy and safe way by doing nothing. Risking nothing, he lost nothing. The master was looking for effort, a willingness to try, and the confidence that one's best would be good enough. This third servant did not understand his master, and the poor fellow was tossed aside and called wicked and lazy.

The Lord likened the work of God to rain and snow that water the earth, producing bud and seed and crop:

So shall my word be that goes out from my mouth: it shall not return to me empty, but it shall accomplish that which I purpose. (Isa 55:11)

The word became flesh in Jesus, according to John's Gospel. God is determined that the word/flesh achieve the purpose for which it was sent: putting us into action. The action is varied and obvious; there is enough for everyone. On the streets of Calcutta, if a dying street person can teach a young German volunteer about love, then none of us are beyond the simple doing of something that is good. All of us are not called to be heros or martyrs, successful or famous, earth shakers or leaders. We are simply offered the example of Jesus who always found something to do.

When I was in seminary, a professor announced that each student's final grade would be negotiated between the teacher and student. As I sat down in my professor's office, he asked me what I deserved in the course. "I'd like an A," I said somewhat confidently. He actually smiled a friendly smile. "Why do you think you should get an A?" I was ready with a good reason. "Well, sir, I have never gotten an A before, but I have never worked harder before in my life. So if I have ever deserved an A, it is now." My professor wrote something in his book, then looked at me. "Do you suppose we could settle for an A-? Everyone can always work a little bit harder."

In considering what Jesus teaches us about work, the same principle applies. We are expected to do our best, and we can always do more. He asks nothing more of us than he gave himself. Jesus chose the hard way to Messiahship: He worked for it. He broke the rules, did what he could, kept a beautiful attitude, worked with integrity, stayed focused, invited others to share the work, kept his spiritual center healthy, and kept an eye open for something else that needed doing. If the principle of faith at work ever has a trademark, it will belong to Jesus the Christ.

Chapter 5

—The God-Provider—

I described this book to a friend and shared concerns about the nature of work nowadays and reflected on some feedback from a speech on the subject. My friend summarized my thoughts with terminology from his sales work in textiles: "FUDS." It stands for fear, uncertainty, and doubts. Whenever FUDS is on the increase, jobs are on the decrease. FUDS inhibits aggressive action toward growth and results in a "circle the wagons" mentality in such a hasty way that a lot of wagons do not make it into the circle.

Faith at work is meant to be an antibody for FUDS. If FUDS drives the economy to distraction, renewed ideas about and dedication to work can bring us back to the center. More often than not, FUDS rules the day. The only certainty in the economic future is uncertainty. As we close out the twentieth century and prepare to embark on the twenty-first century, no one is quite certain about the job market or economy. Two reasonable people in a room will express quite opposite predictions.

In chapter one I mentioned the competition between Japan and the U.S.A. that is becoming increasingly nasty and filled with name-calling. People need someone to blame for economic woes, so Japan is a ready target. The whole issue of a world economy and its impact on regular folks befuddles most of us. NAFTA is a good example.

The North American Free Trade Agreement sounds wonderful—or demonic, depending on who speaks. America's number one conservative radio talk show host favors it; the number two man is against it. Bush and Clinton are for it; Perot is against it. One company promises that NAFTA will create jobs, while another corporation threatens the loss of jobs. The only certainty is uncertainty. People are so concerned about jobs that NAFTA is either looked to as the Messiah or the home-wrecker.

As the debate about NAFTA heated up before the congressional vote, America was treated to live debate on the Larry King show between Vice President Al Gore and the third party contender in the 1992 presidential election, Ross Perot. Full page ads, paid for by different interest groups, screamed out at American citizens as they read the morning paper at breakfast. Foreboding commercials warned American T.V. viewers in the evening of dire consequences if their view did not prevail.

The *Washington Post* seemed to provide the most sane approach. The 26 October 1993, edition included an indepth advertising supplement titled "NAFTA Yes." The 27 October edition provided the same coverage under the banner "NAFTA No." In both editions politicians, business leaders, bankers, and experts touted their various statistics and arguments to make their point. While some space was saved for discussion of other issues such as NAFTA's impact on the environment, U.S. sovereignty, immigration, and the economy in general, the main thrust was jobs.

Jobs, work, and employment—this is the mantra of the day. Perot talked of the giant sucking sound of jobs escaping to Mexico, and others warned of losing 500,000 jobs or more immediately. Companies such as TOYS 'R' US weighed in with ads noting that "eighteen out of nineteen independent economic studies predict that NAFTA will increase overall American employment."[1] Over $10,000,000 were spent on television, radio, and newspaper advertising, lobbying the voters for one side or the other. Unlikely bed fellows emerged, with Congressman Newt Gingrich and President Bill Clinton working together in opposition to Ross Perot and Jesse Jackson. Only the non-identical twins—hope for jobs and fear of losing jobs—could sustain such debate, interest, emotion, and money.

Given the certainty of uncertainty, the best solution for our spiritual and mental health is not to allow ourselves to be defined by our employment. We do not gain our identity or meaning from the source of our paycheck. Faith at work simply affirms that joy, purpose, meaning, satisfaction, and happiness can come from any endeavor, direction, or activity in which God is affirmed.

People often ask one another, "What is your profession?" The answer we give is usually defined by our workplace, paycheck, or boss; so we answer with the title of our job or the name of our company. In an economy where job security and satisfaction are increasingly rare, however, putting faith to work offers a different answer: "Me? Oh, I profess that God is love, God loves you, and God loves me; so I spend my time helping others to know God's love." Or, "My profession is a God-provider. God is love, so I provide God to anyone I can."

God-provider—a great job whether NAFTA fails or succeeds. As the economy slows or revives, with a world economy or subsistence farming, there is always plenty of work for God-providers. We had better grab the opportunity because good full-time work is hard to find and harder to keep!

Lars-Erik Nelson, a syndicated columnist featured in *Newsday*, tells us about Charlie, the C.E.O. of a Fortune 500 Company. To Charlie,

> his employees are not employees. They are not people. They are FTEs
> —"full-time equivalents." Charlie's goal: Have as few FTEs as possible.
> When the corporation bought a major-league baseball team, Charlie—or
> so the story went—was handed a diagram of his new "cost center." He
> studied it for a moment and then asked, "Why do we need this FTE be-
> tween second and third base when we don't have one between first and
> second?"[2]

In an atmosphere that turns people into FTEs, where the noblest goal is to reduce FTEs, and where even shortstops are considered excess baggage, it might be wise to look elsewhere for long-lasting satisfaction and job fulfillment! Making a profession as a God-provider might lessen the stress of having one's self-worth defined by a heartless FTE counter.

The alternative of faith at work is to allow your life to be defined by God, who values every ounce of energy you expend as surely as God counts every hair on your head (Matt 10:30). You are intrinsically valuable to God, as stated in Jesus' teaching in Matthew 10 and 6 where we are told several times, "Don't worry!" The opposite of worry is confidence. The opposite of an FTE is a person created in God's own image, worthy of Christ's loving sacrifice on the cross and entrusted with the privilege of being a God-provider to others.

Jesus said to "forget worry and the objects and actions of worry." Our focus should be on the kingdom of God and its righteousness (Matt 6:33). When our self-worth comes from the pursuit of the Kingdom, and when we define ourselves by the joy of being God's own person full time, no one can take our contentment away.

Growing up in the 1950s and educated in the 1960s, I was under the assumption that people found work when they finished school, stayed with one company or profession until retirement, and lived happily ever after. On college campuses, graduating seniors were wooed by company representatives in an atmosphere not unlike fraternity rush. There was a mystique about such companies as IBM or Kodak. A job with one of them meant a person was set for life.

This mystique is now gone, replaced by cynicism, fear, and even betrayal. In the spring of 1993, Johnson and Johnson, an attractive and reputable company, announced that—despite excellent profits—it would cut its work force by 20,000 people to prepare for the future.[3] One might assume that the work ethic of those 20,000 people had something to do with the company's productivity and profitability, but nowadays that does not even guarantee job security.

The 26 July 1993 issue of *Newsweek* provided a case in point with Proctor and Gamble. Despite "a raft of top-selling, high profile brands . . . and its (high) potential for growth overseas,"[4] the news for Proctor and Gamble was grim. *Newsweek* reported:

> In the halls of Proctor and Gamble headquarters in Cincinnati, he's known as the "Wrecking Ball." And last week, CEO Edwin Artzt struck with a force that left the venerable packaged-goods company shaking on its foundation. Artzt announced that the 156-year-old manufacturer of everything from detergents to disposable diapers would eliminate 13,000 jobs and close 30 of its 147 manufacturing plants over the next three years.[5]

Perhaps the most cynical view of the American labor market appeared in Jim Barlow's article in the *Houston Chronicle*.

> During the 1990–91 recession, 56 percent of American companies laid off almost a tenth of their employees—actually, it averaged out to 9.6 percent. In the economic recovery year of 1992, some 46 percent of all companies laid off a little over a tenth of their work force—an average of 10.4 percent.

Welcome to the new American economy. The old days of hiring on with a company and staying with it for the rest of your life are gone. Smart companies that want to get good work out of you will still treat you well while you are needed—giving fair pay and benefits, a decent work environment, and things like that—but when they can do your job cheaper, you are gone.

The northeast United States, New England especially, was hard hit by the recent events in the economy—recession, readjustment, transition to a peace economy, downsizing, or whatever we call it. The *Boston Sunday Globe* took a poignant look at the results in human terms. Bruce Butterfield wrote in the 10 October 1993 edition,

Like survivors of war, many full-time workers today are nearly as ravaged as their fallen comrades—drained of loyalty to a system that, to them, is collapsing all around. They are not enjoying life as much as hanging on to it—often by the tips of their fingers.

After nearly a half-century of rising wages and living standards, the clock is being rolled back even for those who have kept what had been good full-time jobs. Workloads are increasing, incomes dropping, benefits disappearing.

But more debilitating than the loss of a pay or reduced health benefits, the full-time jobs many hold today no longer carry any sense of security or cooperation. One slip, one lost contract, one change in the global marketplace or corporate policy or ownership, and even the safest of work is suddenly on the line—even at companies where productivity is high.[7]

Butterfield cited AT&T to symbolize the bizarre nature of today's workplace. In 1992, AT&T's manufacturing plant in North Andover was celebrated as "one of the most productive and progressive workplaces in America." Seven months later, nearly 1,000 jobs were cut—20 percent of the work force.[8]

A survivor of several downsizings at Digital spoke with dread,

Waiting for that tap on the shoulder, I have dreams where I come into work, and my entire area is roped off with those yellow police lines, like a police crime scene. I'm saying, "I've got to get into my office. I've got to get my daughter's picture. Can't I have that?" And they're saying, "Get out. You don't belong here anymore!"[9]

Butterfield went on to list workers' declining weekly earnings, the devaluation of people, threats of automation and cheap labor abroad, and the demand for profits at any cost as contributing factors to the battlefield mentality.

Butterfield told a "war story" about an ex-Digital employee:

When Frank Giaramita, now forty-four, joined Digital fresh out of college, he found he wasn't working for the computer company so much as marrying it, and that it was married to him. When he and his wife, Diana, were involved in an accident on their honeymoon in Mexico, Digital executives from Mexico City quickly appeared on the scene—offering a jet to fly Diana, who was injured, home on the spot.

When Frank decided to adopt Diana's children from a former marriage, the company paid all the costs. That's the kind of organization it was. They wrapped you under this umbrella from the day you became an employee, he says.

But those days and benefits are long gone—washed away in senior management changes designed to turn the economically troubled computer-maker around. Workers understand that. But they don't understand the demise of a cooperative management style that was supposed to be the wave of the future. Giaramita survived the first round of big layoffs, then the second—working longer and harder than ever before, often away from home five days a week.

When he was caught in the recent layoff, he got the word via voice mail from his boss.

"I feel like Scarlett O'Hara in *Gone With the Wind* yelling, 'I'll never be hungry again,' " he says. "I will never, never, give that kind of blind dedication and loyalty to a company again." Nor, he says, will he expect it in return.[10]

Back in the 1960s a folk singer, Eric Andersen, questioned the overall value of the U.S. effort in Vietnam by asking "What was gained for what was lost?" Someday, economists and theoreticians will try to evaluate the benefits and gains of current economic and corporate policies. Will they consider the cost of losing loyalty to and from a company? What is the cost of a labor force turned cynical or a corporate image gone sour? What is the cost of management by fear, intimidation, or nerdicide?

Is there an answer for all this? Since I have spent my life enjoying the fruits of democracy and the free market system, and with my basic understanding of capitalism, I am not suggesting that we scrap it all. I do wonder whether we have taken profitability and turned it into greed. Is it really possible that stockholders' demands are so extreme that companies have no choice but to streamline or excess the very people who helped give them their last dividend? Can we parents only feel fulfilled if our children have it significantly better than we did? If we have two cars and three T.V. sets, is it Christian or even reasonable to equate our children's success with having four cars and six T.V. sets? Is it not time for some new definitions?

The principle of faith at work has helped people to reconsider such basic work-related concepts as weekends, free time, vacation, retirement, and leisure time. By taking it one step further, we can reclaim all of our time and effort for the glory of God and remove them from the cold-hearted judgments of those who worship only the bottom line.

This concept offers at least a partial answer by redefining our paycheck and what constitutes the idea of the worker deserving his wages. While Paul was referring to the church elders (1 Tim 5:18), and Jesus was advising the seventy-two people sent out to evangelize (Luke 10:7), I think we can agree that they both felt that all workers deserve their wages. But is it a wage?

I once was told that everybody wants to be well paid, but we do not always use the same currency. Some persons want to be well paid in dollars. Others want prestige, power, joy, satisfaction, compliments, recognition, promotion, popularity, spiritual merit, and political clout. The list is endless of the ways in which we could be made to feel that a certain effort was worth it.

This idea of payment is precisely the opening for faith at work. Putting one's best on the line for the Lord has its reward. The rewards of joy, satisfaction, and spiritual blessing can make palatable the other work we must do to pay the bills. Putting our faith into our work might even transform our appreciation and experience of those hours and efforts we once accepted as drudgery. The apostle Paul, for example, spent some time as a tent-maker in order to finance the ministry that was his real joy. Tentmaking paid the bills, but serving the risen Christ was the purpose of his life.

I have a dear friend in New York City, Walter Jones, who always tells of how he began his church with six women and thirteen children in rented space above a bar. Walter was a mailman by trade. The U.S. Postal Service claimed his energy five days a week. In return, the federal government put food on his table, clothed his children, and provided shelter for the Jones Family. In his heart, Walter Jones was always a preacher and teacher, a pastor and leader extraordinaire. Today, The Majority Baptist Church owns a whole city block and offers a dynamic ministry under Jones' direction, but for many years, the direction came from a full-time mailman. The key point is that Jones never lost sight of who he was or whose he was. No matter who signed his check, or no matter what claimed five days out of each week, he was still God's man—a pastor and preacher of the Good News. The postal service employed him, used him, and paid him, but never owned him. This example demonstrates one way to put our faith into action.

Faith at work also offers a relationship and product that is long lasting. If job security is to become a thing of the past, we do not have to give up our hopes for security. A God-provider—one who serves God with every ounce of energy and lives an active Christian theology of the obvious—is a lifelong, full-time job. There is no lack of work. God's kingdom is a right-to-work kingdom. If you are willing to do it, there is plenty to be done.

When President Clinton took his first summer vacation, every detail became public knowledge. After his return to Washington, in an address to a gathering of clergy, Clinton revealed that a major part of his vacation reading had been Stephen Carter's book, *The Culture of Disbelief.* Carter argues for, and Clinton affirms, the reintroduction of religious devotion into the mainstream of American discourse. Indeed, the subtitle of Carter's book suggests that religion has been "trivialized" in weighty areas such as law and politics. He goes so far as to suggest that in much of America, God is just "a hobby," not something or someone to be taken seriously.[11]

Carter challenges us to let our spirituality matter, to make it count, to be intentional about bringing our faith into the daily arena. His ideas reflect the principle of faith at work. Whatever you do is important to God. Therefore, offer it to God. Let each moment and activity be God's; sacralize it. This way, your whole life is lived in God's employ, where there is never any lack of work.

With God, there is permanence and security. A few years ago, I was asked to organize a chapter of The Fellowship of Christian Athletes (FCA) at my son's high school in Georgia. FCA attempts to help athletes understand the correlation between doing one's best for Christ and doing one's best on the playing field. The elected president of our FCA chapter, Toby Rush, was a superb athlete. He was all-league as a football tail back, basketball guard, and baseball short-stop. One afternoon, I asked him why it was important to him to be part of FCA. His life seemed so full, active, and successful that one more meeting almost seemed too much.

Toby knew his spiritual playing field even better than he knew the baseball diamond. He told me,

With God, I am number one; I am always number one. I know that I might fumble away a big game, or hurt my knee and never play basketball again, or make an error with the bases loaded, and the people in the stands will turn against me. They'll boo me; to them I'll just be another bum. But not with God. God will never turn on me. With God, I am always number one, so I want everyone to know that God is number one with me.

Toby's commitment represents the standard employee contract with God. Allow God to be number one in your life; allow yourself to be number one with God. Experience true security.

I have become interested in Qawwali music, which is Sufi Islamic music of a most fervent and mystical style. One of Qawwali's great singers is Nurat Fateh Ali Khan of Pakistan. In an interview, Mr. Khan said,

When I perform, I feel that the poetry is for my God, and I feel nearer to God. Whenever I have a concert that went wrong, I check the four elements—heart, brain, throat, and voice—to see what happened. But God gave this gift, so I really don't have too many bad nights.[12]

This singer echoes his faith at work. When whatever we do is done for God, it is almost always excellent work.

I was given excerpts of an interesting book called *Dedication and Leadership*[13] by Douglas Hyde. For the most part, it is a scathing attack on communism, but the author also looks admiringly at certain qualities that enabled communism to gain such power. Hyde argues, for example, that the early communists had success in attracting workers precisely because they saw work as the best place to bring their communism. Unlike so many Christians who have somehow bought into the idea that we should leave our religion out of the workplace and confine it to the home and church, the communists saw the workplace as the ideal place for "evangelism."

Hyde tells the story of attending Mass on Easter Sunday at a church on the edge of a southeast Asian jungle.

The sermon had already just begun when I arrived. An old Indian priest was preaching to a congregation of Indians and Chinese, the majority of whom were very poor. He told them that the women on the first Easter Sunday went looking in the garden for the risen Lord. They looked in the tomb, and they did not find him there. They looked around the garden; again they could not find him. But, said the preacher, "You do not have to look in a tomb; you do not have to look around a garden to find the risen Lord. He is in your hands. When you go out to work tomorrow, whether you are riding a trishaw, or digging a drain, or whatever you may be doing as your daily work, you will be cooperating in God's work of creation. God is in your hands."

Sitting in front of me was an old Indian coolie with gnarled, bare legs, around which varicose veins entwined themselves like creepers on a branch of a tree. As the preacher said the words "God is in your hands," I saw the old man look at his toil worn, calloused, twisted hands and broken nails, almost in awe. Something tremendous was happening to him. Throughout the rest of the sermon he looked, time after time, at the hands which had suddenly taken on a new sublime significance. His work, whatever it was, would never be the same for him again. Suddenly, no matter how degraded that work might be, it became meaningful for him. His Christianity suddenly became relevant to his work. Or, to turn it around the other way, his work suddenly linked to his beliefs so that God and religion would no longer belong just to Mass on Sunday. His beliefs could be related to cleaning the monsoon drains the next day or pedaling away from morning till night on a heavy trishaw.

That, of course, is how any Christian should see his work. This is one of those obvious things. But it is not necessarily how Christians do see it. If they did, the so-called "Christian West" would be very different from what it is. The values of Sunday mass or service would be taken to the stock exchange, the board meeting, the marketing campaign office, the factory, but quite evidently, they normally are not. For the Christian and for most others, work is divorced from belief.[14]

Faith at work precludes such a divorce. Once we dare to think of theology and work together, we do away with the compartmentalization of life into secular and sacred that has bedeviled (now that is a good choice of a word!) Christians for too long. If everything is God's, and God is omnipresent, we simply cannot carve out a large segment of our life such as work and then put up a sign warning God, "Do Not Enter!"

Consider the dilemma of Dr. Larry Dossey. Dossey, an internist and chief of staff at a large hospital, wrote the book *Healing Words*. He was caught between the scientific edge of medicine and a growing awareness of the spiritual benefits of healing. He studied 100 experiments that sought to document any relationship between prayer and healing. One study included 400 coronary care patients in which those persons who had been randomly selected to be prayed for without their knowledge had better than average healing results.[15]

In an interview with Peter Steinfels of the *New York Times,* the dilemma was described: As a physician committed to scientific evidence, could he withhold from his patients a form of treatment that he increasingly believed was efficacious? Was he ethically obliged to pray for them?[16] Remember, Dossey's question was from the perspective of a paid worker. Of course, a clergy person can offer to say a prayer with a patient, but what about a hospital employee—a Medicare or Blue Cross reimbursed expert, a skilled specialist? Dare he keep such God-work as prayer overtly out of the workplace?

We cannot keep God out of the workplace. We can legislate against it, deny it, or ignore it, but we cannot enforce it. God is in the workplace. God is in the obvious. Shall we join our force with the God-force to become a spiritual work force? Shall we find the satisfaction, security, continuity, and fulfillment that our innermost being seeks from work? Or shall we simply cower with fear in the face of downsizing, nerdicide, new economic reality, and so on?

Perhaps the distress obvious in this chapter shows that I have a poor grasp of economics, but I fail to understand why we should equate good business practices with personal cruelty. It is said that all politics are local. All firings, layoffs, and golden parachutes are also local. They hurt real people with real families in real towns. We can try to hide them in annual reports or bury them in the obscure pages of the business section, but somewhere real people are really hurting.

Evidently in the name of "good business," anything goes. It is no wonder that secular business, free of the constraints of Christian ethics, feels free to attack the work force with a butcher's glee. What else can explain the following reports about Xerox?

A headline of the 9 December 1993 issue of the *New York Times* read, "A Profitable Xerox Plans to Cut Staff by 10,000." My local newspaper, *The Berkshire Eagle*, explained,

> Xerox CEO, Paul A. Allaire, said the restructuring is not a defensive move, but instead an attempt to intensify the company's efforts to

improve productivity. He cited the company's third quarter results, when
Xerox reported a twenty-four percent increase in profits.[17]

If a company's profits go up by twenty-four percent, is it good business to hurt 10,000 real families that helped produce the profit? Again,
we are left to ask the question: "From where shall we get our joy, fulfillment, and identity?"

I am not denying the value of work. Believe me, when I was out of
work for two years, I was glad to find a job! Certain family matters of
security, health, education, and shelter came into sharp focus during that
period, and we breathe easier now that those matters are not threatened.
Yet, this era is not the time for allowing our identity and self-worth to be
tied too closely with the name of the employer who signs our paychecks.
Faith at work suggests that we look inward and upward for our satisfaction—not outward to the supervisors, employer, or workplace.

Bernard Kouchner founded two organizations that are literally on the
front line of worldwide human and natural disasters: Doctors without
Borders and Doctors of the World. His work has been lauded, applauded,
and awarded, but Kouchner keeps a simple perspective: "People are
bleeding," he says. "I stop the bleeding."[18] His philosophy embodies faith
at work, the theology of the obvious—doing what you can with what you
have where you are.

Kouchner also brings an ethical and philosophical perspective to his
work. It emanates from something inside that he feels and enjoys as a
runner. Just before the 1992 New York City Marathon, he told an inter-
viewer,

> When I see runners gathered like this today, it seems to me a symbol
> of what can be done. War is the worst side of humanity. Running is the
> best. And let me tell you, most of the people making war are not run-
> ners. It would be a better place if they were.[19]

Imagine if Christians felt as positive about the effects of their faith
and spirituality on the world as Kouchner. Imagine if we actually believed that our spiritual discipline could produce just as astounding
results as an athlete's discipline. Imagine if we believed the Ten Commandments (what we do not want others to do) and the Two Great
Commandments (what Jesus tells us we had better do). Imagine if we

affirmed Paul's emphasis on faith and grace with James' call to do good works. Imagine if we lived our Sunday morning faith all week long.

William Barclay, writing in *God's Young Church*, borrowed a story from Leslie Weatherhead:

> There was a young girl dying in a London hospital. She was literally tired to death. Her parents had died when she was very young, and she was the eldest of the family, and she had actually worked herself to death looking after her younger brothers and sisters.
>
> A visitor came to the hospital. The visitor was one of these hard people with no sense of what is kind and Christ-like. The visitor said to this girl, "I suppose you know you're dying. What are you going to do when you go to stand before God?" The girl just did not know. The visitor went on. "Were you ever baptized?" No, the girl's parents had never thought of that. "Did you ever go to Sunday School or church?" No, she had been too busy looking after her younger brothers and sisters for that. "Then," said this bullying visitor, "What are you going to do when you go to God?"
>
> For a moment or two the girl did not say anything; then she looked down at her hands lying on the white coverlet of the hospital bed. They were all rough and red and hacked with the work that she had had to do; and she said softly, "What am I going to do when I go to stand before God? I think I'll just show him my hands."[20]

This story combines the best that our beliefs about work have to offer. She did what she had to do. She did what was obvious. Her work and faith were so interwoven as to be indistinguishable. She poured herself out on the playing fields of life. There was nothing left. When her life was over, she was done.

What was her profession? Maid? Chief cook and bottle washer? Martyr? Nanny or baby-sitter? No, she was a God-provider. Her theology may have been sketchy, and her tool was probably a soup kettle, but she gave the love of God to her brothers and sisters in a way that few of us could match. Hers was a workable theology.

Endnotes

[1]Advertisement, "For Once We're Asking You Not to Believe in Fairy Tales," *New York Times*, 12 November 1993, A13.

[2]Lars-Erik Nelson, *Newsday*, Op-Ed.

[3]Radio news report. Source unknown.

[4]Anetta Miller, "No Cheers for Proctor and Gamble," *Newsweek*, 26 July 1993, 38.

[5]Ibid.

[6]Jim Barlow, untitled, *Houston Chronicle*.

[7]Bruce Butterfield, "Work in the 90s," *Boston Sunday Globe*, 10 Ocotober 1993, 1.

[8]Ibid.

[9]Ibid., 22.

[10]Ibid., 23.

[11]Stephen Carter, *The Culture of Disbelief* (New York: Basic Books, Harper Collins, 1993).

[12]Nurat Fateh Ali Khan, with Peter Watrous, "Virtuosity as a Vehicle to a Higher Realm," *New York Times*, 12 November 1993.

[13]Douglas Hyde, *Dedication and Leadership* (South Bend IN: Notre Dame Press, 1966).

[14]Ibid.

[15]Larry Dossey, *Healing Words* (New York: HarperCollins, 1993).

[16]Peter Steinfels, "A Doctor Looks to Science for Proof of a Spiritual Realm," *New York Times*, 19 December 1993, E7.

[17]"Xerox to Cut 10,000 Jobs, Close Plant," *The Berkshire Eagle*, 9 December 1993, D1.

[18]John Hanc, "Healing the World," *Runner's World*, December 1993.

[19]Ibid.

[20]William Barclay, *God's Young Church* (Louisville KY: Westminster Press, 1970) 35-36.

Chapter 6

—Visible Christianity—

Christians must make the connection between faith and works, religion and practice, and believing and doing. This connection should be obvious and visible so that even the casual observer cannot miss it. Applying faith at work can make the relationship unmistakably clear.

For the principle of faith at work to be anything more than one more sermon from James ("faith without works is dead"), it must call people to a full integration of work, play, worship, and study. If such integration is absent, theology becomes only an intellectual pursuit, and good works become merely works. Each needs the undergirding and strengthening provided by the other.

Why not let every good work be a theological statement and every theological effort be an act of love? It seems that western civilization led the way into carving life into segments such as work, fun, charity, and religion. Western religion found such segmentation comfortable. Therefore, religion is what we do on Sunday mornings, work is what we get paid for during the week, fun is what we do on the golf course, and charity is whatever we spend that is tax-exempt. Perhaps our society has found such divisions profitable, and religion has prospered (in a worldly sense) by cooperating. I prefer the worldview in which our relationship with God permeates our daily life and intrudes into every nook and cranny of our existence.

Years ago Charles Sheldon wrote a popular book called *In His Steps*,[1] which offers a similar premise. In it the pastor and congregation of a successful, comfortable, suburban church are confronted one Sunday morning by a desperately poor man who dies in their midst. Their final, well-intentioned efforts to help him are too late. Some people in the church are shaken by this experience and choose to enter into an experiment. What if they were to live every day, confront every issue, and reach every decision according to just one ethical standard: What would Jesus do? The book follows the efforts of various church people as they try, failing some days and succeeding on other days. At work, at the club, on the street, in the home, or wherever—the question pushed them: What would Jesus do?

God challenges us to take the whole person into every activity. Even some enlightened businesses are seeing the benefits of such an integrated, holistic view of work. Day-care centers, health club facilities, stress management courses, support groups, and spiritual and psychological counseling can now be found on site with some companies.

The ABC evening news reported on an experiment with some corporate executives. During a week-long seminar, they role-played a typical American assembly line putting together a simple gadget. This method emphasized each worker remaining stationary and doing the same task over and over, while parts and products piled up before and after his or her work station.

After two days, the executives were introduced to the ways of their most dreaded competitors, the Japanese. For two days, they role-played a Japanese style, called "flow manufacturing." They worked together in concert with other workers, plugging in wherever they were needed, moving from one assignment to another. This method provided the opportunity to the worker for valuable interaction. It also increased productivity and worker satisfaction. One corporate leader remarked, "Usually, the worker leaves his brains at the factory gate when he comes to work. Now, we are inviting the whole person in."

Inviting the whole person in could be a slogan for evangelism and faith at work. We are invited by God to bring our whole person to the table, office, playing fields, classroom, and sanctuary. We are invited to be whole people all the time, not divided. Jesus put it simply in the Sermon on the Mount:

> No one can serve two masters; for a slave will either hate the one and love the other, or be devoted to the one and despise the other. You cannot serve God and wealth. (Matt 6:24)

God is not a part-time God. We do not want God working in our behalf only part-time, and God does not want us working part-time for God. We expect God to be on the job full-time, providing just the right balance in the world so that life goes on and opportunities abound. Likewise, God expects us to be working full-time in God's way, God's style, and God's spirit.

This does not mean that we become unproductive, monastic, or devoid of all comforts and leisure and joy! Quite the opposite. In fact, Jesus follows the challenge to us to choose once and for all whom we shall serve with a section of scripture designed to set our minds at ease:

> Therefore, I tell you, do not worry about your life, what you will eat or what you will drink, or about your body, what you will wear. But strive first for the kingdom of God and God's righteousness, and all these things will be given to you as well. (Matt 6:25, 33)

Jesus invites us to choose God as our master, seek after God's kingdom and righteousness, and bring our relationship with God into every activity of our lives. The end result is that the needs of our lives, the very reasons we work, will be satisfied. If all of our work is God's work, then we are God's workers full-time, and we will more fully appreciate the benefits of our full-time God.

The corporate world is already beginning to understand the benefit of "inviting the whole person in" that Jesus predicted two thousand years ago. Faith at work only seeks to increase the benefit. When the world of work invites us to bring our brains as well as our brawn to the work station, the employees stand to be astounded when we bring our hearts, souls, and spirituality along.

Are we comfortable making our Christianity visible, integrating our faith fully into our daily lives, taking our spirituality out of the relative privacy of our worship center and into the more public arena of work and play? In fact, some might wonder if this suggestion is dangerous and un-American.

What happens if "visible Christianity" is followed by "visible Judaism" and "visible Islam"? We need this kind of spirituality in our daily lives—not dogma, creeds, doctrine, or conversion. The visible Christianity that I advocate is its spiritual essence, the things that unite and strengthen people, not the religious/denominational issues that divide. While I am not an expert, I am a student of world religions enough to welcome their spirituality as a benefit, not a danger. But, again, is this invitation to "visible Christianity" un-American?

The United States has a well-deserved passion for the concept of separation of church and state. After all, several of the original states were founded by people fleeing religious persecution. Unfortunately, religious intolerance managed to make it to the shores of America as well. The separation of church and state seeks to assure that people's petty bigotries will never become official policy. In effect, religion and politics agree to non-interference in each other's affairs. The government will not run the churches, and no church or religious movement will be favored by the government or permitted to dictate to the government.

Through the years, the concept of church and state separation has remained lofty, but the practice borders on the absurd. One rule of politeness states that when people get together two topics are forbidden (especially at the dinner table): politics and religion. Here are two subjects that can, on the one hand, and should, on the other, envelope our lives. Yet, discussing them is put in the same category as burping or telling dirty jokes!

Indeed, the government should neither rule over the Church nor favor one church over another. We do not want the institution of any church to be dominated by, toyed with, manipulated by, or favored by the government. But a biblical belief system about work is not an institution, a structure, a hierarchy, or a political entity. At its best, it should move people who have internalized their Christian faith so thoroughly that it is a natural part of everything they say and do in their waking hours.

My friend Azariah took me to visit Swami Ranganathananda in Hyderabad, India. The Swami is the third generation leader of a movement that has tried to share the insights of Hinduism with the world. He was very hospitable and shared humorous and interesting insights into America, travel, religion, and Christianity. Above all, I remember one of his closing comments:

> I do not wish to make everyone into a Hindu. I just hope that something
> I say might make a Methodist a better Methodist, a Catholic a better
> Catholic, a Jew a better Jew.

Swami Ranganathananda did not view his message as competitive or incompatible with other positive, God-affirming messages. I feel the same way about a belief system about work that is properly constructed, holistic, and fully integrated. Its goal is to so thoroughly spiritualize our every effort that we become better employers and employees, volunteer coaches and scout leaders, tennis and bridge partners, church and civic leaders, and soup kitchen and food pantry volunteers. The concept of faith at work challenges us to believe that every time we use our energy is a spiritual exercise.

The popular rock group "Police" sang a song of concentrated energy with these promises:

> Every breath you take,
> Every move you make,
> Every step you take,
> I'll be watching you.[2]

We consider such lyrics to be romantic. From God's perspective, they represent spirituality. Faith at work dares us to devote every breath, move, and step to the fulfillment of God's hopes for this world. Work, play, school, sports, charity, relationships, and even romance require our energy. We can give them our best; our least; or our halfhearted, inbetween effort. Our best is heart, soul, mind, and body.

When I was a young pastor, I was blessed with an outstanding layman in the congregation, Olin Salmon. He was a man of great faith and humility—devoted to family, church, and community. When he retired, I attended a joyous celebration in his honor. As we sat together during dinner, he turned to me and said, "David, I have wasted my life. The summer after high school, I walked into the hardware store and never left, and now it's fifty years later."

Mr. Salmon was equating the value of his life with the job description of running a hardware store in a small town. At the end of his life, it did not seem like he had contributed much. Hardware was not Olin Salmon's life, however. It was the source of his income. It provided the mortgage, food, and an education for the kids. Olin's life's work was people. In every aspect of his life, he put people first and made others his priority. As a scout leader, church moderator, neighbor, businessman, citizen, and family man, he represented a set of qualities and convictions that made a genuine difference in the life of so many persons.

I quickly changed the focus of my banquet remarks to say, for Mr. Salmon's benefit, that his life was not hardware, and his work was not over. I hastened to emphasize the importance of owning a hardware store, but that it just was not the sum and substance of his work-life. In fact, the reason that people would honor a retiring hardware store owner is because he was the same man in or out of the store, during and after work. His humility, generosity, fairness, and Christianity permeated all aspects of his life. If he had cheated customers in the hardware store, no one would have wanted him as a scout leader. If he had been cruel in business, he never would have succeeded as a church moderator. If he had abused his family, no one would have trusted him in the community. With Mr. Salmon, however, everyone knew they were getting his best, the best that his Christian faith could generate in his daily life.

Paul urged us to be "persistent whether the time is favorable or unfavorable" (2 Tim 4:2). This verse is just a poetic way of telling us to be dependable, reliable, and constant in our Christian faith. People should not be able to distinguish between when we are in our working mode and when we are in our Christian mode. Athletes talk about putting their "game face" on—when they become grim, serious, hard, tough, and competitive. We cannot expect a linebacker, who is paid to crush other people, to act like a linebacker all of the time; but God expects that we will make every effort to act like a Christian all of the time. God does not expect us to have a "Christian game face" that we take off and on when it is convenient.

Does being a Christian full-time make us weaker, poorer, wimpier, or less effective? Do we lose our competitive edge, or are we less able to be counted on for good work if Christ remains important to us even at work? This debate is popular within professional baseball. A few years ago the San Francisco Giants were a mediocre to bad baseball team. Critics traced their demise to the presence of too many Christians on the team. Evidently, if a relief pitcher gave up a home run and lost the game, he would say, "It was the Lord's will." If a batter struck out with the bases loaded, he did not take the blame; he thought it was God's will.

Such talk is foolishness, if not blasphemy. It is certainly diametrically opposed to the image of God who is the author of "every perfect gift" (Ja 1:17) and who demands the very best from each of us. My own experience with baseball is that God seems generally disinterested in the outcome. I am certain that God is a baseball fan and equally certain that God is a New York Yankee fan, but God is not a manipulative puppeteer pulling the strings necessary to gain a strike-out, home run, or victory.

I do believe that God is virtually interested in how the game is played—the game of life as well as the game of sports. Whether we are competing on a playing field or in an office, whether it is business or pleasure, whether with family or friends or strangers, God is so intimately aware of us that the very hairs of our head are numbered and known in heaven. We are to take Christ onto the playing field and into the workplace, permeating the classroom and family room and influencing the halls of governments and streets of our towns. Faith at work has no limits or boundaries. It is meant to go everywhere. It also gives a different meaning to accomplishment and success.

I once asked a businessman, "What is the morality of what you are doing? Don't you ever stop to ask yourself if this is good or bad?" He became defensive and furious as he retorted, "Don't ask me such a question! You have no right to expect me to decide or choose anything on the basis of what is moral. I haven't got time for that."

I do not entirely blame this fellow. Making moral decisions, taking into account what is right and wrong, weighing good and evil—all take time and are hard work. If people get paid only to produce a good bottom line, then this is the ultimate good that counts. This person seemed convinced that seeking the moral good and doing the right thing would make him appear weaker, wimpier, and less effective. But by what standards, and by whose definition?

The Bible answers this dilemma a hundred times. Jesus said,

> For what will it profit them if they gain the whole world but forfeit their life? For the Son of Man is to come with his angels in the glory of his Father; and then he will repay every one for what has been done. (Matt 16:26-27)

The challenge for the Christian is not to profit by gaining the world, but by keeping the soul. All too easily we have determined that winning at any cost is the only goal. It was said of the ancient Spartans that the only sin was in getting caught. Everything else was permissible. This particular perverted ethic now threatens to win our so-called Judeo-Christian society.

One morning I heard a radio ad for a car dealership. A man with a mocking Japanese accent begged the listeners to buy used or new Japanese cars in order to make Japanese workers happy. The fake and insulting Japanese voice urged people not to buy a certain American-made car because it was made by lazy American workers. I drove immediately to the dealership to register my protest for the tasteless and racist ad. The man responsible for the ad campaign was proud of the ad and the results, however, and was suspicious of me. "You can't be an American," he shouted. "Where are you from? Did you drive here in a Toyota?

Where were you when Pearl Harbor was bombed? This is all about Pearl Harbor. Our sales are up 200 percent since the ad started." Sales were up, and he was winning; nothing else mattered.

Perhaps our definition of winning has become warped. The Bible is certainly not against winning, triumph, or victory. Paul, in writing about the great joy of Easter, expressed it in the language of winning:

> Death has been swallowed up in victory! Where O death, is your victory? Thanks be to God, who gives us the victory through our Lord Jesus Christ. (1 Cor 15:54, 55, 57)

To the same audience of Corinthians Paul wrote,

> Do you not know that in a race the runners all compete, but only one receives the prize? Run in such a way that you may win it. (1 Cor 9:24)

Victory and prizes are okay to pursue, but they do not come easily. They are not awarded prematurely, nor are they given for short-term effort. Paul understood the need for a long-term strategy that would carry to ultimate victory, not a quick fix. To Timothy he wrote,

> I have fought the good fight, I have finished the race, I have kept the faith. From now on there is reserved for me the crown of righteousness. (2 Tim 4:7)

What a contrast to those who seek easy solutions, popular decisions, short-term profits, and care nothing for what is moral or good! Jesus told us to forget gain or profit and concentrate on keeping our soul. Paul told us to keep our eyes on the real prize, finish the whole race, and keep our faith alive.

The scriptures also reveal what our ultimate goal should be. Paul calls it a "crown of righteousness." Imagine if all of our efforts were in pursuit of righteousness! Why can't Little League coaching, soup kitchen cooking, building houses with the poor, operating a business, going to school, playing on a team, or being a church all be committed to righteousness? But would righteousness hamper the work we do? And, if so, should we be doing it?

If the only way to succeed at what we do is to keep our Christianity invisible, then we should look seriously at what we are doing and if it is costing us too much in the long run. If the way of Christ is so important to us, we run the risk of being unrecognizable when the time comes for our ultimate job performance review. According to Luke's Gospel, it will not be an easy review with Jesus:

> Someone asked him, "Lord, will only a few be saved?" He said to them, "Strive to enter through the narrow door; for many, I tell you, will try to enter and will not be able. When . . . you begin to stand outside and to knock saying, 'Lord, open to us,' then . . . he will say to you, 'I do not know where you come from.' " (13:23-25)

Jesus encourages us to choose the narrow way even if it does not appear to be as easy, popular, or profitable as other ways. On judgment day the real bottom line is whether or not God recognizes us, based on whether or not we made the right decisions.

God is definitely interested in winners and winning, but God has a narrow definition of what is worth winning and a narrow set of guidelines as to how we go about winning. The prophet Isaiah gave a mostly forgotten description of this Messiah that we claim to be Jesus:

> Here is my servant whom I uphold, my chosen, in whom my soul delights. I have put my spirit upon him; he will bring forth justice to the nations. (42:1)

The Messiah, our Jesus, is to be the winner. He is to be victorious in the area of justice. He is the Messiah, triumphant over death and leading justice to victory.

Spike Lee, the African-American filmmaker, urges us to "Do the Right Thing." The Apostle Paul urged us to run for the prize, keep the faith, and receive the crown that comes from righteousness. One of the starkest descriptions of the Messiah emphasizes an ultimate commitment to justice. This Jesus urges us to live a life and make decisions that will enable us to be recognizable as God's own.

Suddenly, the idea of visible Christianity takes on a great urgency. Invisible Christianity leads to those troubling words, "I don't know you." Visible Christianity opens the narrow door, leads justice to victory, and earns the crown of righteousness.

Before we demand too much of those who work, paid and volunteer, in the secular world, we must be honest with how difficult it is to practice visible Christianity within Christian settings. In the local church, we expect and accept that religion, faith, and spirituality will have a significant role to play during worship, Sunday School, and midweek services.

If a person attends one hour of worship, one hour and fifteen minutes of Sunday School, and one hour of midweek worship or Bible study, he or she has spent a total of three hours and fifteen minutes in overt, visible, obvious Christian living. What about the rest of the week? Before we can consider the more difficult question of living a visible Christianity during forty hours of paid work, we must start with making Christianity visible in the rest of our church life.

Consider committee meetings, board meetings, trustees meetings, church council, and even fellowship and fund raising activities such as the annual church fair, bake sales, bean suppers, and maybe even Bingo! Here the difficulty begins. If we cannot figure out how to carry over our Christianity from a Sunday School class to a Tuesday night diaconate meeting, what hope do we have of ever presenting a Christian presence at the office or the plant or in the classroom? If we who worship God on Sunday cannot continue our unity in love during the church fair later the same week, how can we ever think of making a difference in the workplace the next day?

In short, a desire to be Christ-like cannot be turned on and off. Paul often likened the Christian life to an athlete. The excellent or serious athlete is always in training. In the same passage where Paul urged us "to receive the prize," he added,

> Athletes exercise self-control in all things. . . . So I do not run aimlessly, nor do I box as though beating the air; but I punish my body and enslave it so that after proclaiming to others I myself should not be disqualified. (1 Cor 9:25-27)

I am not an excellent athlete, but I am a lifelong athlete. When I was younger, I competed in a variety of sports. Now, I will play baseball with my son and a little one-on-one basketball. Mostly, I am an everyday runner, covering three to five miles. During the autumn, when Aaron competed in 5K road races, I would enter a race just to see how I compare to other middle-aged runners.

Even with this low key, athletic involvement, I fully comprehend Paul's advice on strict training and the need to "punish my body and enslave it." I realize that everything I do directly affects my performance as a runner. Once I became a serious (visible!) runner, I took everything into account. Eating, drinking, and sleeping, and when, what, and how much—all of these issues had a direct bearing on my running. Late night snacks, a large breakfast, insufficient sleep, and any amount of donuts seriously changed my ability and desire to run. Everything I did directly affected not only the physical act of running, but also how well I ran and how much I enjoyed it. Now, after years of serious running, running determines everything from schedule to diet.

Paul told us to take the same lessons learned from athletes and apply them to living our lives as Christians. Serious, visible Christians will not take a week, weekend, or night off. Their Christianity is not a fad, hobby, or side interest. Instead, it has become a part of their identity, or something that defines them.

Visible Christianity merely calls for our faith to be the defining spirit of our lives. It is our essence—who we are, how we act, and what we do. In visible Christianity, we cannot separate our faith from any facet of our lives without feeling it, confronting it, being uncomfortable about it, and wanting to do something about it. Visible Christianity seeks a reintegration of our spiritual life with our daily life.

Visible Christianity affirms that our faith is so important to us that we just naturally take it wherever we go. Like the athlete who desires a consistent, credible performance and will not do anything to jeopardize his or her ability, the serious Christian lives a lifestyle so visible in commitment to Christ that it overrules every other aspect.

Faith at work is the practical application and theological outcome of visible Christianity. As we become defined by our commitment to Christlikeness, we will inevitably bring Christ into every arena in our lives. With Christ visible, alive, and real in every ounce of energy we expend, we reach the goal of faith at work. All that we do becomes our offering to God: Our space becomes sacred space, our work becomes sacred work, and our lives become "holy and acceptable to God" (Rom 12:1).

In the age-old debate between evangelism and social action, this bridge ends the struggle to decide whether we should live out our faith on one side or the other. Visible Christianity is enlightened evangelism that lives its faith proudly and overtly, without arrogance or self-righteousness. Faith at work is spiritualized social action that does its good work without being embarrassed to name the carpenter who leads us. Together, the good works are more assuredly good, our walk matches our talk, and everyone benefits.

Endnotes

[1]Charles Sheldon, *In His Steps* (Old Tappan NJ: Fleming H. Revell Co., 1967).

[2]Sting, "Every Breath You Take," Syncronicity, A & M Records, 1983.

Chapter 7

—Call to Action—

Perhaps one of the most basic, crucial questions about the nature of spiritual life is whether or not it is active or passive. This question exposes one of the major weaknesses of Christian debate. Why do we so often insist on answers to spiritual questions being at one extreme or another?

For example, twentieth-century Christianity has been divided into two camps: evangelicals and social activists. Evangelicals emphasize evangelism, telling the Good News of Jesus Christ. Social activists, followers of the Social Gospel, emphasize doing good. At the risk of gross generalization, too often the evangelicals have avoided doing good, and the social activists have avoided including God in the program or credits. Such division gives rise to a warped view of what it means to be a Christian.

God calls us to a full range of spiritual activities such as personal and private acts of devotion, worship, piety, offering, prayer, and study. We are called upon to meditate and reflect. We are invited to take our prayer life into the isolation of a closet. We are even invited to privatize our charity in such a way that our left hand will not know what our right hand is doing (Matt 6:3).

There certainly is a place for quiet, intimate, passive Christianity. The Psalmist knew how valuable it is to stop whatever we are doing in order to hear and feel what is truly important: "Be still, and know that I am God" (Ps 46:10). While sheltered in a cave, Elijah discovered the same truth when he encountered God. There was thunder and lightning; the heavens put on a magnificent show of power.

> He said, "Go out and stand on the mountain before the Lord, for the Lord is about to pass by." Now there was a great wind so strong that it was splitting mountains and breaking rocks in pieces before the Lord, but the Lord was not in the wind; and after the wind an earthquake, and after the fire a sound of sheer silence. (1 Kgs 19:11-12)

Elijah was told that the Lord would come near him. He expected something majestic, grand, spectacular, and dynamic. The Lord was not in all the events that would seem to correspond with the presence of one known to be almighty, however. Instead, God was in a silent voice.

Quiet piety in our spiritual lives is certainly needed. There is a time for retreat, refreshment, and reflection. Yet even in the military, the purpose of retreat is simply to regroup in order to be more effective in the next attack. Retreat is not surrender. Unfortunately, Christianity is too often a totally passive experience. Worship is too often a spectator sport at best. The preacher and the choir perform; the congregation sits back, listens, and usually leaves behind what it hears.

God wants even our most passive endeavors to be strategic preparation for serving God in active ways. The passive parts of our spiritual life are not God's work in and of themselves; nor are they what we do before we work. They are all God's work. Faith at work provides this holistic perspective. It seeks to elevate the practical. Even the most pietistic part of our spiritual life can be practical. Indeed, it can be the practicality of piety and spiritual life that makes it come alive.

I once attended a retreat on meditation led by a Catholic nun. She brought us into the sanctuary and had us get comfortable, sitting or reclining around the alter area. Pillows were provided. Then we were asked to close our eyes. After a period of silence, she read John 21, the story of Jesus' post-resurrection appearance to the disciples on the shore of the Sea of Galilee.

In this familiar story, as the disciples fished, Jesus appeared incognito. He advised them to fish on the other side of the boat, a successful venture. Then the disciples recognized Jesus and joined him on the shore for breakfast, and Jesus told Peter three times to feed the sheep if Peter really loved him.

The story was nice, but the nun took us deeper into our meditation by emphasizing the practical and obvious, the real aspects of the story we might miss in our typical attempt at being passively spiritual. She asked us to experience the whole scene: to see the boat and wear and tear on the nets; to feel the sea breeze and even the occasional spray of water from the waves; to hear the wind blowing, the waves lapping, and the chitchat of the fishermen; to smell breakfast cooking over the open fire on the beach.

Incredibly, the whole story came alive. It was real. I was there. I could feel it. It was no longer just a collection of scripture verses. It was the living Word, the word made flesh and dwelling among us (John 1:14). Once enticed into living and breathing the very scripture I was hearing, I had a front row seat for one of the most dramatic moments in the life of Christ.

Jesus turned toward Peter—brash, bold, and filled with arrogance—the first to affirm Jesus as the Messiah. Just days before, he boldly refused to have his feet washed. He pompously announced that he would never deny Jesus. Peter alone went to the sword in defense of Jesus when Jesus was arrested, but could not stay awake while Jesus agonized and sweated blood in Gethsemane. He would not even admit to knowing Jesus and denied Christ three times in the courtyard. He apparently could not bring himself to go to Calvary, show his face, express his love, or just be there. When the women announced the resurrection, Peter's reaction was to ridicule them.

The nun had invited me to feel the breeze, hear the waves, smell the cooking, and place myself there on the shore of Galilee. Her instructions did not seem to be particularly holy, pious, or spiritual. To the contrary, such obvious particulars as the mundane details of the fishermen's morning ritual might seem to detract from the other-worldly holiness we expect of spirituality. Instead, I found myself privy to one of humankind's greatest conversations, as found in John 21:16:

> "Do you love me?"
> "Lord, you know that I love you."
> "Tend my sheep."

These words could have been written on a page or taken from scenes of a film on the life of Christ, but I had the chance to be there—thanks to the invitation to experience intimate, practical, active spirituality.

I could feel the tension in the air, the anxiety, and the questions. Peter's embarrassment and humility were obvious as Jesus' eyes penetrated into the heart of the disciple. Jesus' questions were pointed and poignant. Peter's answers were honest and confident. The swagger, false pride and macho posturing were gone. Jesus was satisfied. Betrayal, resentment, disappointment, fear, shame, and doubt were defeated. Repentance, forgiveness, blessing, calling, renewal, hope, and faith took their place. I was there.

Faith at work does not value the practical over the spiritual anymore than it values volunteer labor over paid labor. This concept calls for an end to either/or options. It argues for devoting and consecrating all of our efforts to God. Quiet piety and spiritual activism and volunteerism and professionalism are all needed if Christian people are truly to respond to God's call.

God calls us to action. The call may come as a whisper or as a silent voice as heard by Elijah, but even the whisper can be demanding. God calls us to a journey on a path that is risky, courageous, and dangerous. How do you think Christianity acquired so many martyrs? In generation after generation, nation after nation, Christians suffered and died for their actions. Whether they stood for or against something, at least they were standing!

Again, these thoughts are not a diatribe against piety, quietude, reflection, silence, or any of the gentler aspects of Christian life. I am suggesting that the purpose of all spiritual life is to be drawn closer to God, and the inevitable result of getting closer to God is discovering very clearly what God wants. We can retreat to be with God; but if the retreat is successful, we will burst forth from the experience with the conviction that "faith, if it has no works, is dead" (Ja 2:17). Works are the consequence of faith. Christ-centered activism is the consequence of spiritual passivity. Your living faith will put you to work. If you "take time to be holy," as the great hymn advises, you will find yourself very active.

Consider fasting. Outwardly, nothing could be more passive. It is a spiritual discipline that is affirmed throughout the scripture. At its simplest, fasting is absolutely passive. Greater minds than mine have called it a spiritual discipline and speak of practicing denial. Practice and discipline require concentrated effort. Fasting, in the truest sense, is work. Unfortunately, fasting usually becomes just one more ritual that folks go through because it is expected. Jesus relaxed this requirement of fasting when he made fun of people who put on long faces and made themselves appear to be suffering in order to draw attention to their spirituality (Matt 6:16-18). Fasting is not for self-glorification, but for purification. Biologically, it is a cleansing of the body. As a spiritual act, it requires putting aside routine desires and habits in order to concentrate on God.

Mahatma Gandhi made an art of fasting, renewing it as an intensely spiritual act with direct socially activist results. He linked the spiritual discipline of not eating with demands for an end to violence and oppression. Passivity in self-denial carried the clout of massive action and intervention in behalf of God's goals of justice and mercy (Mic 6:8).

Isaiah also tried to set the record straight on fasting. Isaiah 58 ridicules and condemns the sinful abuse of fasting by so-called righteous people.

> You serve your own interest on your fast day, and oppress all your workers. You fast only to quarrel and to fight and to strike with a wicked fist. Will you call this a fast? (vv. 3-5)

People fasted to show how holy they were, but their behavior was just as miserable. Perhaps they even excused their rottenness by citing the irritability that comes with being hungry. God would have nothing to do with such a fast. In God's behalf, Isaiah offered a whole other view of this seemingly passive spiritual device.

> Is not this the kind of fasting that I choose: to loose the bonds of injustice, to undo the thongs of the yoke, to let the oppressed go free, and break every yoke? Is it not to share your bread with the hungry, and bring the homeless poor into your house, when you see the naked to cover them? (vv. 6-7)

Consider the verbs in these verses. They do not express passivity but require action—"oomph," doing something, expending energy, being aggressive.

I was once asked to preach the Good Friday service at an ecumenical gathering in Indiana, Pennsylvania. My message was entitled, "God Is a Verb." Verbs always carry the action. They are the doers, movers, and shakers of every sentence. Verbs can even stand alone in a sentence. Nouns cannot stand alone. They may be subjects or objects; but standing alone, they lack vitality, purpose, and direction. They need to be brought to life and moved to action.

God is a verb. God is. God does. If our spiritual life succeeds in bringing us closer to God, we will find ourselves face to face with a verb. The modern church can debate whether God is male or female, but God acts and sounds like a verb. We may argue the gender of verbs, but the purpose of a verb is clear: to carry the action.

The importance of deliberate action is noted in these thoughts from John W. Harvey and Christina Yates:

> God is not a personage who orders us to prostrate ourselves before Him
> —a radically false position—but one who says: "Stand up, here is my
> task for you; take it and get on with it." God does not require incense
> from us. What he does require is that we should listen and take action—
> the true response of love.[1]

Something about God causes us to pause. According to Nehemiah,
Daniel, Zephaniah, and the Psalmist, our God is an "awesome God."
God's awesomeness moves humanity to worship, devotion, and piety, but
these acts constitute only half of the fitting response to God. Through the
ages, worshiping people have mastered the art of acting reverent, awed,
and appropriately humble. Yet, God is not satisfied with our half-hearted
attention. Look at what God said about worship, life, and action through
the prophet Amos:

> I hate, I despise your festivals, and I take no delight in your solemn
> assemblies. Even though you offer me your burnt offerings and grain of-
> ferings, I will not accept them. . . . I will not look upon them. Take
> away from me the noise of your songs; I will not listen to the melody
> of your harps. But let justice roll down like waters, and righteousness
> like an overflowing stream. (5:21-24)

God is not opposed to the passive side of our spiritual lives. The God
who speaks in the small voice of a whisper, who challenges us to be still,
who affirms the qualities of the Beatitudes, and who turns passive resistance into a spiritual strength is a God who welcomes prayer, meditation,
hymn-singing, Bible reading, and other forms of personal piety.

Three thousand years ago, God was already fed up with those who
drew near to God but refused to listen, who went on retreat but never
regrouped to attack, who kneeled for prayer but never stood up for anything, who made generous offerings inside the church but never offered
anything of themselves elsewhere, and who sang spiritual songs but lived
empty lives. Today an exasperated God shouts, in effect, "Forget the self-
serving fluff that makes you feel better. Give me justice and righteousness pouring out of you, or give me nothing!"

God calls us to action, not in place of a spiritual life, but to complete
our spiritual life and make it whole. Putting faith to work affirms the
wholeness of the Gospel. It is not in place of the theological efforts to understand the nature of God. It merely says that to fully understand God,

we need to hear God calling us, and, invariably, God calls us into the arena of a hurting world.

Some years ago, a seminary conducted an experiment. Students in a preaching class were assigned different times to show up at a certain place to give a sermon. Half of the students were required to preach on the parable of the good Samaritan. The other students were free to choose their own topic. The students were also given specific instructions on the path they were to take to the assigned classroom. The path included a narrow alley way in which a man was lying who looked the part of a person in great pain and need of urgent care.

One by one these future preachers of the Gospel walked the path, confronted with the man in desperate need. The results only confirmed the exasperation that God expressed through the prophet Amos. Busy, hurried, and perhaps nervous about the sermon they had to preach, these students managed to avoid dealing with obvious need right in front of them. They passed by on the other side, squeezing up against the wall or stepping over the victim. Even with the parable of the good Samaritan fresh on their minds, with the sorry example of religious leaders neglecting to care for the biblical victim, the students rushed to their pulpits.

I cannot be harsh in judging these students. My greatest shame would be to count all of the people in need that I neglect every day of my life and all of the opportunities I miss to let justice and righteousness flow. Faith at work is a wake-up call to look around and see the missed opportunities.

When Jesus healed the blind man in Bethsaida (Mark 8:22-26), he touched the man. "Can you see anything?" Jesus asked. "I can see people, but they look like trees," the man responded. The world did not need one more person who could look at people and not see them for what they were. So "Jesus laid his hands on his eyes again; . . . and he saw everything clearly."

God calls us to see people clearly. Their needs, hurts, sorrows, joys, and celebrations call for our response. To put our faith to work, we must go to our tool chest and get the right tool for what needs doing.

Millard Fuller looked at shameful, decrepit shacks and called for an army with hammers and saws to meet the need. Mother Theresa saw dying people abandoned in the streets and babies abandoned at her doorstep and called for people to come who would love increasingly. A British T.V. journalist went into Ethiopia in the 1980s and sent out terrifying pictures of a generation dying of starvation in a world of plenty. The rock n' roll star Bob Geldoff called for guitarists, drummers, and keyboard players to answer the call of the world for help.

Other needs are not so spectacular, but they are just as obvious—if we would accept Jesus' second touch and see people clearly. From your tool chest you may need to bring out a smile, a check, a hammer, a soup ladle, a petition, a call to 911, an hour to spare, a visit, a friendly word, a strong stand, a public statement, a private encouragement, a risky decision, an unpopular choice, a non-violent protest, your vote, your hobby, your talent, or your dream. These and hundreds of other tools are the tools needed to put faith to work. Everything we have and do is offered up for God's use. If we have the means, if we have the ability, if we think of a need or believe in it, the tool is made available to God for action.

Endnotes

[1]John W. Harvey and Christina Yates, "Prayer and Action," *Hymns for the Family of God* (Nashville: Paragon Assoc., Inc., 1976) 410.

Chapter 8

—Local Theology—

Tip O'Neill, the late and legendary Democrat from Boston and former Speaker of the House, is credited with the proverb, "All politics is local." He was saying that no matter what the worldwide ramifications of an issue might be, politicians must ultimately face the voters back home who decide whether or not their interests have been represented. Lofty sentiments and compassionate votes must make sense to the electorate.

The same test should apply to theology. All theology is local. In this effort to propose a work theology, it is essential for it to be useful by those who struggle each day with work. The challenge of a theological statement is to be both truthful and relevant—to be right and make sense to those who hear it.

My beliefs about work emerges from my own experience, an approach often affirmed by two of my theological mentors, Gabe Fackre of Andover Newton Seminary and Orlando Costas, the late Dean at Andover Newton. From them I learned the need to think theologically and allow my life story to impact and be impacted by the truths of Christian faith.

If all theology is local, then it needs to speak to where I live: Pittsfield, a city of 50,000 people nestled in the Berkshire Mountains of Western Massachusetts. Like similar cities throughout New England, Pittsfield was once a company town. General Electric once employed over 12,000 people, providing work for at least one third of the families in the city. Across the border in Schenectady, New York, it was also the mother lode, employing 40,000 people at its height and about 9,000 today.

With the decade of the 1980s, such companies faced downsizing, layoffs, plant closings, and mergers. In less than a year, General Electric in Pittsfield became, in large part, Martin Marietta and then Lockheed Martin as the defense industry giants merged to fight the effects of downsizing in the national defense budget. Such mergers create uncertainty for thousands of people as positions are eliminated in new structures.

On 30 August 1994, General Electric announced the elimination of 1,000 jobs at its Schenectady plant. As a result, many of our church members have moved to the Schenectady plant; and other Pittsfield workers, laid off at their home plant, found work over the mountain and commuted.

By all reports, these individuals were all good, hard, and reliable workers. In 1993, the company challenged the employees to drastically increase productivity in order to save jobs in the Schenectady plant. The 31 August edition of *The Berkshire Eagle* reports that

> Schenectady workers increased productivity twenty-three percent in 1993. The division had record earnings in 1993, . . . and it would have had double-digit earnings growth again in 1994 and 1995.[1]

So what is the hope if a worker does all that is expected of him or her, and profits are realized handsomely, yet the specter of the pink slip only increases?

Our local newspaper chronicled the work life of one General Electric employee. Mark Rivers is thirty-five years old, a lifelong resident of the area, and a graduate of the machinist's course at our city's vocational high school. For ten years, he worked in the power transformer department, and then moved to ordnance (weapons) when the other work closed shop. That change took him from a simple ten-minute commute in Pittsfield to a Schenectady trip that can take two hours in the winter. But now, what does the future hold for Schenectady, with the promise of 1,200 layoffs lurking around the bend?

Life is lived in small steps when one is always on the verge of losing a job. Rivers thought he might be among those "laid off in October, but probably should make it until February, or possibly June. . . . When you work for G.E., you are never safe."[2] In the meantime, his family's dreams of a house will have to wait. Perhaps he will survive this cut and the next one and work happily ever after. He has already learned, however, that his identity, hopes, and joy cannot be dependent on a large company keeping him just to be nice. He contributed his fair share to increasing productivity and enlarging profits, but in the modern work world that is not enough.

The concept of faith at work is not only local; it is personal. It must speak not only to America, or to the 1,200 people laid off in Schenectady, but to a single individual like Mr. Rivers, saying, in effect, "You're O.K. God loves you. You're doing a great job with your kids. You have contributed well to the community and beyond. Keep your chin up. Be proud of who you are. There is still work for you to do."

Faith at work reminds us that not only must we be ready to find work elsewhere, but we most certainly must find our meaning, satisfaction, and identity elsewhere. The sum and substance of who we are cannot be what we do, where we do it, or for whom we do it. Our essence cannot be something that can be taken away by a layoff, a merger, an unappreciative supervisor, a surly boss, or an unfair salary or performance review.

God's own self-definition states, "I am who I am" (Exod 3:14). Can we be so bold as to stand tall in defense of who we are?

One of the essential questions of any theology is "Who am I?"— Who am I in relation to God, others, the world, and the act of salvation on the cross? Who am I when it comes to work, effort, meaning in life, paycheck, and family and community responsibilities and activities? Who am I to my employer, supervisor, co-workers, and employees?

Dietrich Bonhoeffer dared us to stand boldly before the world and let the world take its best shot at defining who we are. He stated in his *Ethics*:

Ecce homo!—Behold the man! In Him the world was reconciled with God . . . not by its overthrowing but by its reconciliation. It is not by ideals and programs or by conscience, duty, responsibility, and virtue that reality can be confronted and overcome, but simply and solely by the perfect love of God . . . the really lived love of God in Jesus Christ . . . . It experiences and suffers the reality of the world in all its hardness. The world exhausts its fury against the body of Christ. But, tormented, He forgives the world its sin. *Ecce homo!*[3]

Bonhoeffer presented a new humanity made possible by emulating the life, values, and work of the very real Jesus of Nazareth. Repeating the refrain, *"Ecce homo!"* Bonhoeffer reminded us that Jesus' greatest work was to embody "the unfathomable mystery of the love of God for . . . the real world"[4] and in that great love to totally redefine our standard of success.

Ecce homo! Behold the man sentenced by God, the figure of grief and pain. . . . In a world where success is the measure and justification of all things the figure of Him who was sentenced and crucified remains a stranger and is at best the object of pity. The world will allow itself to be subdued only by success (which) alone justifies wrongs done.[5]

Then, in a scathing attack on the worldly successful he sadly warned,

When a successful figure becomes especially prominent and conspicu-
ous, the majority give way to the idolization of success. They become
blind to right or wrong, truth and untruth. They have eyes only for the
deed, for the successful result . . . dazzled by the brilliance of a successful man and by the longing in some way to share in his success.[6]

What is the alternative? To stand erect—before God, neighbor, family, stranger, and boss—as a person firmly loved through the cross of
Christ, "a sentence of mercy that God pronounces" on humanity.[7] This
is a glorious affirmation that who we are is not based on what we do,
where we work, or how successful we are at our work. Our identity is
based solely on God's decision to place upon us the highest possible
value.

One of the most bizarre twists of legislation in 1994 was an attempt
by the EEOC to regulate religious harassment in the work place. As I
traveled the roads in the spring, listening to talk radio, I heard about the
draconian measures the government was planning to take in order to control, if not eliminate, religious expression at work. For once I found myself in agreement with the anger and frustration expressed on talk radio.

While most people would agree that it is wrong for a person to use
work time to promote their own religious activities, or for an employer
to subtly or not so subtly lean on an employee to entice that person to
attend the boss' church, or to impose one's religious views at a staff
meeting, the suggested EEOC legislation threatened to go much further.
The wearing of a cross or yalmuka or skull cap, the placement of a Bible
on a desk, God talk on a coffee break, the offer to remember someone
in prayer after hearing distressing news—all of these activities could constitute religious harassment.

By late 1994, the chances of the enactment of such regulation seemed
remote. Yet, the ongoing struggle to determine how much one's spiritual
life can impact on work life continues. What would have happened if the
legislation had become law? What if you could not show or express in
any way your religious faith while on the job? Would you, in effect,
cease to be a Christian for those hours when you are on the payroll?

Our Christian faith is not limited to wearing a cross, carrying a Bible,
or praying aloud. If anything, we might be forced to find more real ways

to genuinely express the Good News of the Gospel. When Jesus was asked to exercise more control over his followers during the Palm Sunday celebration, he told the Pharisees, "If they keep quiet, the stones will cry out" (Luke 19:40).

The real Good News can never be silenced. The Good News of God's love has nothing to do with the kinds of religious accessories that are permissible at work. The Gospel has to do with our response to God and how we choose to live as if God has made a difference in our lives.

A friend has begun to work at home after twenty-five years of reporting to an office. He still has the same job and responsibilities, but with modern technology he can carry them out just as easily at home. Working at home is a growing trend across the country. Many people have expressed to me their sole reason for doing this: I like it because I can be myself.

They do not say that they can be *by* themselves, just that they are free to be themselves. Does that mean they can wear their favorite tee shirt and not shave, or walk around in fluffy slippers until noon? Such comfort is a very small part of it. Being themselves at home means no office politics, no backstabbing, no little white lies, and no pretense. At home we have the freedom to be comfortable with who we are and to be ourselves.

The call of faith at work is to learn to be yourself away from the comfort and privacy of your own home or church, temple, or mosque. The hope is that faith might so permeate our being that the prohibition against wearing a cross or carrying a Bible would not diminish the obvious presence of Christ in our lives one bit. Paul tells us that

> The fruit of the Spirit is love, joy, peace, patience, kindness, goodness, faithfulness, gentleness, and self control. Against such things there is no law. (Gal 5:22-23)

In other words, even the federal government cannot legislate against what it really means to live and work as one of Christ's own. You can take the fruit of the Spirit into the workplace, the union hall, the staff meeting, or the performance review. It is easier to be gentle, good, and patient at home; or joyful, loving, and self-controlled in the sanctuary; but we can prove our worth at work if we will be bold enough to try.

The nature of work in the foreseeable future is obviously in transition. Robert B. Reich, U.S. Secretary of Labor, said in a speech:

> Since last Labor Day, the economy has generated more than 2.5 million jobs for Americans. But despite this progress, long-term trends are splitting the old middle class into three new groups: an underclass largely trapped in center cities, increasingly isolated from the core economy; an over class, those in a position to ride the waves of change; and in between, the largest group, an anxious class, most of whom hold jobs but are justifiably uneasy about their own standing and fearful for their children's futures.[8]

Reich's evaluation is not a comforting picture for those who draw their only satisfaction and hope from company loyalty, job security, or the climbing of a corporate ladder.

Correctly, Reich sees some hope in education and retraining:

> The forces unleashed by technology must be mastered, not merely buffered. As increasingly capable machines join Americans at the workplace—join them as both co-workers and competitors—the payoff to education and training has soared, and the penalty for lacking skills has stiffened.[9]

Just as we may need to be retooled for future use, however, we can be reinspired in the use of our energy so that we can feel productive, vital, necessary, and fulfilled in all that we do. This is the contribution of faith at work.

As life and work change, God remains the same yesterday, today, and tomorrow—guaranteeing full employment, great benefits, eternal security, and great rewards. But first we must decide who we are and whose we are. In the shifting sands of work, we need to find an anchor.

In my own life's journey, I have seen my stock rise or fall whenever how I was identified would change. This was true not only for how others viewed me, but for how I thought of myself. Over the years, I have been the associate pastor of a large church, the pastor of a small and struggling church, the senior pastor of a large and distinguished urban church and of an historic suburban church, the pastor of a little house church, and then the senior pastor of an active and respected church in a popular tourist area. Even writing the description of each church betrays how I was seen and how I saw myself.

But was I a different person as I moved from church to church, or could I carry with me the essentials of my faith wherever I went? By essentials, I refer not to the underlying creed of my preaching and teaching, but to the evidence of God's "unfathomable love" as I lived it in the reality of the world in all of its hardness. Could I—from place to place and time to time; working under, with, for, and above a whole range of people; earning from too little to more than enough to just getting by—show myself as one sentenced by God's mercy to be loved?

What about other shifts in our identity? For most of my adult life, I was known for what I did and what I accomplished, and my children were known as just that: my children. Then, for three years, I was not a pastor; and for two of those years, I was unemployed. Suddenly, whenever someone at a party, a church service, the mall, or a school function asked what I "did," I fumbled for an answer. To say I was unemployed created one image. To say I was a writer created another. Both were true facts, but entirely false images. Eventually, I created a new identity. Instead of Aaron being known as "Dr. Rowe's son," I immersed myself into activities at his high school and became known as "Aaron's dad." That identity conjured up an image with which everyone was happy, and it worked fine until Aaron went away to college.

So now who am I? Senior pastor of a respected, active, and dynamic church? Husband of Bonnie? An empty nester? A radio talk show host? An author? Or can I find some consistency in my life that gives me pride, identity, and satisfaction everyday no matter where I am, what I do, or what others think of me?

Part of the answer for me is that I am a runner. Every day for the past fifteen years, I have found the time and a place to run. It is an absolute consistency in my life. It is never too cold, too snowy, too busy, too far away, or too anything for me to fit in enough time for a run. No matter what has happened in my life over a fifteen year period, I have faithfully remained a runner.

Can I do likewise with Christ? Is it possible, or am I willing, for Christ-likeness to be an absolutely essential part of my daily life? I cannot imagine a day detached from running. Why, then, should I allow any day to be detached from God? No matter where I go, I take my running gear with me—to conferences, classes, visits, vacations, and meetings.

Why, then, should I leave the fruit of the Spirit behind? I have awakened earlier, shortened meetings, worked harder, and cut out unpleasantness in order to fit in a run. Why, then, should my spiritual life be closeted away or unavailablr or put out of reach? I talk about running, exhibit its benefits, and share the delights of a picturesque or exhilarating new place to run. Why, then, should I be shy about sharing the love of God that is the foundation of my whole being?

The idea that theology, like politics, is local simply means that if my spirituality really is important to me, I cannot leave it behind, check it at the door, or separate it from other significant parts of my life. It goes where I go and does what I do because it is what I am!

In my constant search for resources to strengthen my desire to serve God in all I do, I am quite open to the spiritual experiences and advice of others. Two books that make the same point, though coming from different directions, are *The Blooming of a Lotus* by Thich Nhat Hanh and *One Heart Full of Love* by Mother Teresa.

Thich Nhat Hanh is a Vietnamese Buddhist monk, and Mother Teresa is the renowned Christian worker in Calcutta. For each of them, the key seems to be immersion. First, they seek to be immersed in their spirituality so that there is no discrepancy between who they are, what they believe, and what they do. Second, they are willing to immerse themselves in the world around them. The people, pain, suffering, love, co-workers, environment—we are challenged to enter into all of these.

The Blooming of the Lotus is filled with guided meditation exercises that put you in touch with every imaginable item in life affecting your life, including some upon which you probably never meditated. Leaves, kidneys, feelings, actions, foods, sex, and nature all have their say in our lives—though not necessarily the final say. Thich Nat Hanh writes:

Knowing that by transforming the present,
I transform the past,
I breathe in.
Determined to be mindful and understanding in the present,
I breath out.

Smiling to the present,
I breath in.
Determined to take good care of the present,
I breath out.

Transforming the past by positive present action,
I breath in,
Seeing my present action influencing the future,
I breath out.[10]

To say that all theology is local requires that we live it in the present. The hope of faith at work is that we will be able to smile to the present.

Mother Teresa is just as anxious to see us smiling. In *One Heart Full of Love*, she is asked,

What should we do when suffering comes to us?
Accept it with a smile.
Accept it with a smile?
Yes, with a smile, because it is the greatest gift that God gives us.
What? To Smile?
To smile at God. To have the courage to accept everything he sends us, and to give him what he asks of us with a big smile.[11]

It is not always easy to smile with the work we do. I have certainly seen too many bosses and workers who never smile. As youth sports become more and more competitive in society, volunteer coaches, young players, and parents are smiling much less. When people lose sight of the purpose, even charitable work can become drudgery, political, or big business. There are too many frowns in church life. Therefore, these spiritual mentors call us to remember to smile. If, as the Bible tells us, our "delight is in the Lord" (Ps 1), and if the Lord is part and parcel of all we do, then nothing can take away that smile.

Of course, applying faith at work is not a guarantee of income-producing employment or success by worldly standards in volunteer activity, but it does redirect our perspective so that all we do gives us pleasure. It does not take away the threat of unemployment or the disappointment of a loss. It can protect us from losing our sense of worth and pride in who we are, but it does not do away with misery, mean-spiritedness, or unfairness. Yet it can lead to effort and opportunity that yield a bounty of joy and smiles.

A young man called me to talk about a change in his life. He had been forced by his board members between doing things their way or God's way. When he chose to follow God's leading, he was given two weeks severance and forced to move his family with four kids out of the company house into a trailer. When he called he was joyous and exhilarated. I could see his smiles over the phone as he talked about being liberated. I wish that I could have introduced him to old Dr. Rauschenbusch who wrote in 1914:

> Dead religion narrows our freedom, contracts our horizon, limits our sympathies, and dwarfs our stature. Live religion brings a sense of emancipation, the exhilaration of spiritual health, a tenderer affection for all living things, widening thoughts and aims, and a sure conviction of the reality and righteousness of God. Devotion to the reign of God on earth will do that for a man (woman or child!), and will do it continuously.
>
> The Kingdom of God includes the economic life; for it means the progressive transformation of all human affairs by the thought and spirit of Christ; it involves the opportunity to realize the full humanity which God has put into him as a promise and a call; it means a clean, rich, just, and brotherly life; it means a chance to be single-hearted and not to by coerced into a double life.[13]

One can hardly read these words and believe them without smiling day in and day out!

Endnotes

[1]Associated Press, "GE Eliminating 1,000 Jobs at Schenectady," *The Berkshire Eagle,* 31 August 1994, D1.

[2]Mary Jane Tichenor, "GE's Schenectady Layoffs Scare Pittsfield Survivor," *The Berkshire Eagle,* 1 September 1994, A1, 4.

[3]Dietrich Bonhoeffer, *Ethics* (New York: Macmillan Co., 1965) 70.

[4]Ibid., 71.   [5]Ibid., 75.

[6]Ibid., 77.   [7]Ibid.

[8]Robert B. Reich, "The Fracturing of the Middle Class," *New York Times,* 31 August 1994, OP-Ed, 25.   [9]Ibid.

[10]Thich Nhat Hanh, *The Blooming of a Lotus* (Boston: Beacon Press, 1993) 107.

[11]Mother Teresa, *One Heart Full of Love* (Ann Arbor MI: Servant Books, 1988) 121.

[12]Walter Rauschenbusch, *Christianizing the Social Order* (New York: Macmillan Co., 1914) 113.   [13]Ibid., 458.

Chapter 9

—Good Samaritan and Gandhian Work Theology—

Mahatma Gandhi was murdered for living his faith at work. He chose to live a life in which every iota of his being was consecrated to God. Leading protest marches, traveling the countryside, working the spinning wheel, fasting until violence was ended, meeting with world leaders, staging a strike against apartheid, worshiping privately or publicly, offering nonviolent resistance, writing profusely, affirming the untouchables, being imprisoned, starting an ashram, studying the scriptures, speaking to the masses—all were life activities to Gandhi. He never separated them into work, leisure, and spiritual life.

Gandhi's whole life was entirely integrated, even as he was integrated with the needs and opportunities around him. Because he cared so deeply, he was killed. His final, radical act of love was to love Muslims as much as he loved Hindus, and to be as concerned about the pain in Pakistan as he was about the pain in India. His love was always expressed in action. The enemies of such love in action killed Gandhi.

In New Delhi, India, a park is dedicated to Gandhi's memory. A stone archway at the entrance is engraved with his words:

> Whenever you are in doubt or when the self becomes too much with you, try the following experiment: Recall the face of the poorest and most helpless man you have ever seen and ask yourself if the step you contemplate is going to be of any use to him. Will he be able to gain anything by it? Will it restore him to control over his own life and destiny? In other words, will it lead to . . . self rule for the hungry and spiritually starved millions of our countrymen? Then you find your doubts and your self melting away.[1]

What an image! Gandhi asked that before we take one more step, expend anymore energy, or undertake anymore work, we stop in our tracks until we determine if our effort will dramatically change the life of someone desperately in need.

In Christianity, we have a lofty, well-developed theology. We have thought deeply for centuries about the nature of God, the purpose of humankind, the plan of salvation, and the role of the church. As a result, we claim a God who is One, who is just and awesome and intimately aware of the human predicament; a God who willfully partners with humanity to bring about equity and mercy throughout the world; a God whose love for people knows no limits and extends even to the sacrifice of Jesus to bring about reconciliation between God and people; a God who lifts up the Church as the best way for people to work together to bring about God's kingdom.

How does your life mirror Gandhi's kind of thinking? At every waking moment of our lives, we are about to do, say, or think something. We are constantly on the verge of our next action, idea, project, or plan. Gandhi would ask where our theology fits in with whatever we are about to do next. The world is spiritually and physically starving. People in need are all around us. The world of the obvious is only an arm's reach away. Will your next step make any difference in just one life?

Gandhi's philosophy dares us to question the purpose and efficacy of every step we take. In effect, it challenges us to take upon ourselves one of the attributes of God. The New Testament teaches us that God is love, and we are commanded to be loving. It also teaches that God is so intimately aware of us that the hairs of our head are counted and that even every bird falling from the sky is duly noted by God. If God can choose to be so intimately concerned about each of us, should we not be just as intimately concerned about others?

At the end of Gandhi's life, India achieved independence—but not without a terrible price. India was partitioned, breaking off two large sections to create what is now Pakistan and Bangladesh. There was horrible bloodshed as Moslems sought refuge in the new Moslem-dominated Pakistan, and Hindus fled to rejoin the Hindu-dominated India. Gandhi, who opposed the partition, was broken-hearted by the terrifying violence and vowed to fast until death or until the violence ended.

In the movie, *Gandhi*, a Hindu man went to Gandhi's bedside to surrender his weapons, bring an end to the fast, and confess his own sin. He said, "My son was murdered, and so I have murdered a Moslem." Gandhi's response was compassionate and provocative. "Find a Moslem boy, an orphan whose parents have been murdered, and raise him as your own son. But raise him as a Moslem."[2]

In a world view in which every hair is numbered, and the plight of every bird is accounted for, no injustice is too insignificant to be righted. Something can always be done. We have challenged ourselves for ages with the proverb, "Where there's a will, there's a way." The Gospel truth may be more powerful, however: Where there is God's love, there is a way.

The idea of faith at work implies that within humanity there is the will, motivated by God's love, to do all that is necessary. No goal is beyond us—whether it is feeding the hungry, eliminating shacks, achieving racial harmony, building a lasting peace, getting out the vote, or helping everyone to experience the personal love of God through Jesus Christ. It merely takes the consecrated offering of every ounce of effort in our lives!

Jesus stated plainly, "Be perfect" (Matt 5:48), a command that leaves little room for error! Perfection is our standard and goal. Yet even as Jesus called us to perfection, he continued steadfastly toward the cross, knowing that we never quite make it to perfection. Echoing the challenge of Jesus, faith at work pushes for a Christianity that pervades our whole life. If perfection is our goal, however unlikely, we must seek it in every arena of our lives. It is not something we save just for our overtly religious lives or charitable good works as volunteers.

Gandhi was given the honorific title of Mahatma because the full range of his daily life was lived with the intentional desire to be as perfect in God's sight as possible. Such a world-view is dangerous. Like Gandhi and Jesus, it can cost you your life. It can cost you your job, friends, popularity, comfort, and status quo. It will not cost you your soul, however. Incidentally, Mahatma means "great soul!"

The good Samaritan was an early advocate of putting one's faith to work. The story is simply told in Luke 10:25-37 of how a man was mugged during a journey from Jerusalem to Jericho. The muggers robbed and beat him, leaving him for dead. People who came along and saw the victim lying in the road failed to do anything. Even professional religious people chose to do nothing. Only a Samaritan helped..

The Samaritan was part of a despised, rejected, and outcast group of people. He was an unlikely hero for any story. Yet, despite all the anguish of a lifetime of mistreatment at the hands of other people, this Samaritan retained a reservoir of goodwill in his heart. When he saw the victim lying in the road, he put aside all other concerns. Fear, prejudice, worry about his own safety, the hassle of getting involved, the financial burden—nothing mattered in the face of a simple, urgent human need.

Do you remember what led Jesus to tell the story about the good Samaritan? He had been asked, "Who is my neighbor?" He told the parable to provide a practical theological definition of neighbor: namely the one who helps, the one who does something worthwhile, the one who sticks his or her neck out to be of service, the one who sets aside all possible excuses in order to "Just Do It!"

Jesus' parable shows the need for a theology of work. It is put into modern-day terms in Clarence Jordan's "Cotton Patch" version of the Bible that envisions two modern professional Christians passing by the victim in the road. First came a white preacher, intent on getting to church on time, not wanting to get involved in any embarrassment. Then came a white gospel song leader. He loved the old time gospel songs, loved to be in front of people, and loved the sound of his own voice. Like the preacher, when he saw the chance to do what needed doing, "He stepped on the gas."[3] Stepping on the gas, avoiding responsibility for what we are uniquely in a position to do, or passing by any part of God's creation in need is the antithesis of faith at work.

If we were to choose an anthem for the idea of faith at work, we could not avoid using the great gospel song by popular rap star, M. C. Hammer. The video version begins in the church, then—as the gospel choir builds to a demanding crescendo "Do not pass me by!"—moves out into the neighborhood and beyond to the highways and byways of life.

Who is the "me" that we should not pass by? Jesus said that the ability to be known as a true neighbor is determined by the response to whomever we find in need. He further made it clear that whenever we respond to someone in need, we are directly reaching out to Jesus himself: "As you did it to one of the least of these, you do it to me" (Matt 25:40).

In other words, whenever we stop to help or take the time to care, we are helping and caring for Jesus. Whenever we pass by someone who needs us, we pass by Jesus. If we graft Gandhi's image onto this teaching, then the next step that we take, after pondering the most wretched and hurting person we can imagine, will be serving directly our Lord Jesus Christ.

Christianity will soon be 2,000 years old as a movement, an idea, a religion, and an institution. Its years have been filled with glory and vanity, martyrdom and tyranny, and sacrifice and silliness. Over the course of our history, we have had much cause for pride *and* shame because we have been inconsistent in our witness. Faith at work provides a path toward consistent Christian practice and virtue by affirming the potential holiness and witness of every breath, step, moment, and action of our lives.

We are invited to be God's witnesses, friends, family, and instrument. If we accept the invitation, however, we must accept it as a full-time relationship. Jesus said, "No one who puts a hand to the plow and looks back is fit for the kingdom of God" (Luke 9:62). In its sloppy form, faith at work is just one more theological excuse for workaholism, a spiritual rationale for always having to do something important, but the deeper meaning is that every moment is important to God. We do not have to *do* all the time, but we must *be* all the time.

Earlier, I suggested that God is a verb, calling us to action. Now, I suggest that we are nouns, always being what God needs us to be. I may have created a grammatical whirlwind from which there is no escape! Yet that is the beautiful simplicity of faith at work. There is no distinction between doing and being, sacred or secular, volunteer or paid. We all have an equal chance to be God's people.

When Moses was confronted by the burning bush (Exod 3:1-14ff.), he demanded to know God's name. "I am Who I am," was God's quizzical response. "I just am," God was saying. God just is. Imagine the potential of our Christian faith if it became so profound in our lives that it just was! Imagine a commitment to living God's love that so permeated our being that it defied definitions; no labels would do it justice, no limits could be set, and there would be no apparent beginning or ending.

In considering personal labels, I recall an obituary I read in a Boston newspaper some years ago: "John Smith, Deacon, Dead at 82." The writer of obituaries has the formidable task of defining a lifetime in a brief heading. For all of the efforts of a lifetime, some day our local paper will sum it all up: "John/Jane Doe, Machinist . . . Lawyer . . . Nurse . . . Homemaker." For John Smith, however, the defining characteristic of his life—deacon—was a commitment of service to Jesus Christ.

Deacons were early practitioners of faith at work. In Acts, we read that the Church was enjoying great popularity and astounding growth, which created a logistical problem. Acts 6:1 reports that some very needy people "were being neglected in the daily distribution of food." From the very beginning, the Christian church took seriously the task of providing practical, personal, urgent care to those in need. As the community of believers grew, however, the needs and opportunities for care also grew, and some people were missed. The safety net was not working.

As a result, the disciples established the first board of deacons for the precise purpose of administering the principles of their faith. With the deacons and disciples using their gifts to the glory of God, the early Church was fully dedicated to evangelism and social action, talking and walking the faith, loving God and neighbors, retreat and attack, faith and works, and quiet piety and outward activism. Together they made sure that God's word was taught and done.

It is pleasant to imagine faith at work lifting Christian practice to new levels of effectiveness and involvement, but it is also dangerous. In Acts 6 we learn of overwhelming human need challenging the resources of the Christian community. By verse 4, the plan to have deacons is developed; in verse 5, Stephen is selected to be one of the deacons; by verse 7, the plan is a success; verse 8 describes the especially effective work of Stephen; verse 9 begins with "opposition arose"; and in verse 12, Stephen is seized, arrested, and put on trial. In chapter 7 he is executed.

In the weeks and months following Jesus' resurrection and ascension, Christianity had experienced dramatic progress. The preaching, teaching, and miracles of the disciples drew the attention of the people and powers. There were even some arrests and interrogation. People such as Peter, James, and John were becoming visible, famous, and irritating. Stephen, a deacon, was the first to be killed, however.

The world has always had its share of people who are threatened by God's way, the way of love. They will often tolerate talk, ritual, liturgy, worship, and prayer; but when the talk turns into action, then the forces of evil turn violent. In Jerusalem, two thousand years ago, the power brokers allowed Peter's preaching on Pentecost and could handle the occasional healing of a lame man, but when Stephen dealt with the nitty-gritty of poor people's daily pain and oppression, he had to be stopped. If Christianity started living out its faith, then it had to be defeated before it changed the world.

Because of their vested interest, enemies of a faith at work never wanted to see the world changed. Their power, control, and self-image rested entirely in a status quo where only a select few were at the top. Stephen threatened to treat the people on the bottom of the scale as though they were important; therefore, he was executed.

Under communist governments and other oppressive regimes, worldwide, the same tactic has been used. Churches are permitted, worship is legal, and prayer is acceptable. Good works are prohibited, however. The persons in power are afraid of what will happen if people start living their Christianity with every ounce of effort in their bodies—taking their faith into the streets, neighborhoods, parks, workplace, and the main streets of life.

Gandhi dared us not to take another step until we determine how it will affect the neediest person we can imagine. Jesus was asked how to inherit eternal life and answered by daring us to be the good neighbor Samaritan to someone who is hurting. Stephen became a deacon to insure that no one was without life's necessities. All three of these men were killed for enacting a spiritual life that had practical ramifications.

A fourth proclaimer of faith at work shared the same fate. Dietrich Bonhoeffer, the courageous German pastor and theologian, sacrificed his life in behalf of a Gospel with teeth. Imprisoned by the Nazis, his execution was one of the last direct orders given before Hitler's fall. His book, *The Cost of Discipleship*, truly characterized his life's work.

In his *Ethics*, Bonhoeffer gave a trumpet call to applying one's faith in the world.

> To allow the hungry man to remain hungry would be blasphemy against God and one's neighbor, for what is nearest to God is precisely the need of one's neighbor. It is for the love of Christ, which belongs as much to the hungry man as to myself, that I share my bread with him and that I share my dwelling with the homeless. If the hungry man does not attain to faith, then the fault lies on those who refused him bread. To provide the hungry man with bread is to prepare the way for the coming of grace.[4]

As Bonhoeffer would conclude, there is no evangelism versus social action. The goal of the Gospel has always been to bring the world ("God so loved the world") to salvation. If need, hurt, pain, and loss so overshadow one's existence that he/she can barely think of eternal matters, it is our privilege to open the door to salvation by walking right into the middle of the need.

The popular terminology used to refer to handicapped people is "physically challenged." We need to think of ourselves as "theologically challenged," leaving us to face some obstacles that are more difficult than other people choose to face. Our particular challenge (not handicap) is that, because of God's love, it is physically and spiritually impossible for us to pass by anyone in need. We cannot and will not do it. Some persons will see our involvement as our weakness or handicap, but we will see it as our challenge and opportunity.

Endnotes

[1]*The Words of Gandhi*, Richard Attenborough, ed. (New York: Newmarket Press, 1982) 25.

[2]*Gandhi*, prod. and dir. Richard Attenborough, 188 min., Columbia, 1982.

[3]Clarence Jordan, *The Cotton Patch Version of Luke and Acts* (New York: Association Press, 1969) 47.

[4]Dietrich Bonhoeffer, *Ethics* (New York: Macmillan, 1955).

Chapter 10

—The Final Exam—

My daughter and I had a similar experience in college, though twenty years apart. We each had a final exam from a professor who seemed more determined to uncover what we did not know rather than to cover what we needed to know. Exam questions focused on obscure and irrelevant matters. Obviously, neither one of us was happy with our grade!

Christianity is exactly the opposite. The final exam is very simple. The answers are in the book; they are not obscure, and often the answers are even highlighted in red! Look at the words of Jesus in Matthew 25:31-46:

> When the Son of Man comes in his glory and all the angels with him, then he will sit on the throne of his glory. All the nations will be gathered before him, and he will separate people one from another as a shepherd separates the sheep from the goats, and he will put the sheep at his right hand and the goats at the left.
>
> Then the king will say to those at his right hand, "Come, you that are blessed by my Father, inherit the kingdom prepared for you from the foundation of the world; for I was hungry and you gave me food, I was thirsty and you gave me something to drink, I was a stranger and you welcomed me, I was naked and you gave me clothing, I was sick and you took care of me, I was in prison and you visited me."
>
> Then the righteous will answer him, "Lord, when was it that we saw you hungry and gave you food, or thirsty and gave you something to drink? And when was it that we saw you a stranger and welcomed you, or naked and gave you clothing? And when was it that we saw you sick or in prison and visited you?"
>
> And the king will answer them, "Truly I tell you, just as you did it to one of the least of these who are members of my family, you did it to me." Then he will say to those at his left hand, "You that are accursed, depart from me into the eternal fire prepared for the devil and his angels; for I was hungry and you gave me no food, I was thirsty and you gave me nothing to drink, I was a stranger and you did not welcome me, naked and you did not give me clothing, sick and in prison and you did not visit me."

Then they also will answer, "Lord, when was it that we saw you
hungry or thirsty or a stranger or naked or sick or in prison, and did not
take care of you?"

Then he will answer them, "Truly I tell you, just as you did not do
it to one of the least of these, you did not do it to me." And these will
go away into eternal punishment, but the righteous into eternal life.

When you take the final exam, how will you answer these questions?
Did you, or did you not, do what needed doing when you had the opportunity to do it? This defining question is also the basic definition of faith
at work—a theology of the obvious.

Whether we are in modern America, the Third World, or in-between,
the need and responsibility of the believing Christian is the same: Do
what needs doing when you have the opportunity to do it. This same principle applies to any urgent human need or pressing social issue that cries
out for your involvement. If you can hear the cry, or if you can see the
need, then you are on the road from Jerusalem to Jericho. You can
choose whether to be a religious hypocrite or a good Samaritan.

Putting our faith to work opens the whole world to our tender touch.
Nothing is off-limits, outside our influence, or beyond our reach. If we
can know it, see it, and feel it, then we can do something to help it. The
workplace, family room, playground, classroom, and street corner all
become extensions of our sanctuaries.

Interestingly enough, the corporate world is beginning to think in a
similar way. The 10 June 1992, edition of *USA Today* reported the for-
mation of an organization called Business for Social Responsibility. The
goal of the fifty-five founding companies is to show that "Doing good is
good for business!" Their tender touch is intended to be wide-ranging.
They plan to be involved in environmental and worker safety issues, sup-
porting job creation and urban programs, building and managing low
income housing, and encouraging corporate donations and employee volunteerism. Their vision of a corporate America includes being a "pal to
workers, a friend to the environment and societal change and still
profitable."[1]

The principle of faith at work has somehow sneaked into the board
rooms of at least fifty-five corporations! We are looking for a world that
is permeated with God—not denominationalism or "churchianity" or the
petty divisions of professional religion, but with God. God calls us to
make a difference—to save, help, and change wherever and whenever we
can.

Our tender touch should be felt each day. Ages ago God gave us the Sabbath for rest, with six other days dedicated to work. We have warped God's idea a great deal. Our religious efforts are now disposed of on the Sabbath, and then we ignore God the other six days. The Sabbath is for rest, but all seven days belong to God.

The scriptures also call for a tithe to be given to God. So, to a greater or lesser degree, religious people give an offering to God. This is not to say that we can do whatever we want with the rest of our money. All of our time and money, work and play, and church and society belong to God. Our ability to make a difference in the world is not confined to our free time, volunteer efforts, charitable giving, or church involvement. It extends into each nook and cranny of our lives, from our own backyards all the way to corporate headquarters.

I have long been a student of the literature of India. Among the great literary figures of the world is Rabindranath Tagore of Calcutta, a Nobel Prize winner. In *God-Concept in Gitanjali,* Tony Edacheriparambil explores Tagore's views of God.

> Once Tagore was asked, "You speak a lot about God; are you sure there is a God at all?" Tagore replied in a soft and serene tune, "No, at times I experience the presence of God in depth and touching manner. It is on those moments there emits verse from me. That's all I can tell."[2]

Dr. Joseph Kolagaden, in his foreword, wrote,

> Tagore could see eternity in the grain of palm, in the blade of grass, in the chirp of birds and the sound of the stream, in the dust and din of Calcutta. Where the sky is blue and the grass is green, where the flower has its beauty and the fruit its taste, . . . there is revealed to us the person who is infinite.[3]

Tagore sensed the presence of God in everything and, therefore, refused to limit God by definition or denomination. This view of God as everywhere had a practical application. Kolangaden added:

> The vertical ascent to God is justified only if there is the corresponding horizontal diffusion in service to fellow beings. Consequently Tagore has lashed out at the empty religious rituals that are not in any way related to the promotion of the welfare of the whole creation.[4]

For too long humanity has mastered the art of looking up (the vertical ascent) to communicate with God at the expense of looking around (the horizontal diffusion in service). God called to Moses from the burning bush and to Elisha with a whisper. God calls to us from the beauty of nature and from the cry of the needy. Faith at work says, "Look around; see what is obvious; help out."

In 1983 I began a small ministry with a friend, Mr. K. Azariah of Khammam, India. Our story is told in the book *Something Small for God*, a title that affirms the significance of anything we do if it is for God's glory and not our own. I was attracted to Azariah and his co-workers because they embodied faith at work. They did whatever needed doing whenever they had a chance to do it. They were always looking around.

Azariah is an evangelist by profession and calling. He could be expected to preach, establish churches, and baptize new Christians. For over thirty years he has done these things very successfully, but the traditional activities of an evangelist barely touch the surface of what Azariah does with his life.

I first met him because he wanted to do something about the deplorable conditions in which many of the poor live. Therefore, he organized the first Habitat for Humanity project in India, which has now built over 700 houses. His colleague, Sister Mary Seethama, was distressed by the plight of the poor elderly women with no family. So, together they established the Faith Home for the Aged. When Azariah found several families with leprosy living under a bridge, he put together an effort to build a community for over twenty families.

Sister Mary and Azariah knew a doctor whose eighteen-year-old son —brain-damaged at birth—was helpless. Together with the doctor, they established the Bethel Home for Physically and Mentally Handicapped Persons. The large number of children without resources for schooling, proper nutrition, or health care led to the founding of the Redeemer Christian Center for 150 boys.

If Azariah's ministry group found a village that lacked clean water, a school, or teachers, the members dug wells, built classrooms, and provided teachers. When they prayed with poor people who were sick with tuberculosis and a host of other diseases, they paid for medicine, vaccinations, and hospital care. Confronted by the overwhelming need of people without arms or legs, Azariah's team established artificial limb clinics.

Are such actions the work of an evangelist? If evangelism is the sharing of the Good News, then Azariah's ministry is providing the fullest expression of good news. The job of the team is to preach, teach, represent, exhibit, bring, share, deliver, and be the Good News of Jesus Christ in every way, shape, and manner that their little corner of the world requires.

Azariah's ministry is like kudzu, the whimsical plant of the American South. It grows wherever it wants to go, climbing over trees, farm machinery, and old houses. Whatever direction it needs to go, it goes. Similarly, Azariah's team members are always looking around, alert to new ways through which God can use them, putting their faith to work.

In my book, *Something Small for God*, I describe this approach to ministry as "See a Need, Meet a Need."

> That seems to describe Azariah's view of ministry, life, and mission. One night my daughter, Camaron, and I were at the Khammam train station waiting to take the train to Madras with Azariah. Camaron and I were soon surrounded by a group of young Indian men asking questions, trying out their English. Out of the corner of my eye I noticed Azariah striking up a conversation with an elderly poor woman. I could see him writing out a note, giving her money, summoning a rickshaw driver. He told the driver to take the destitute woman to his house for the night, and the next day she could be taken to our Faith Home for the Aged.
>
> All this took place within a matter of minutes. When all was arranged, I went immediately to Azariah. I was sure I could learn some profound spiritual insight into how to identify need and opportunity. I wanted some easy test, a formula, some prescription for discernment. So I asked Azariah, "How did you know she was in need?"
>
> "I asked her," Azariah answered.
>
> "Why did you go to her?" I asked.
>
> "She was there," he said.
>
> That is a simple prescription for ministry: See a need, meet a need. Open your eyes, look around, ask questions, get to know, offer to help.[5]

For most of the 2,000 years of the history of Christianity, people have been busy trying to make the religion more complicated than it needs to be. We now have creeds, catechisms, doctrines, denominations, hierarchies, and political infighting—all of which detract from the central Gospel. The Gospel of Jesus Christ is incredibly uncomplicated. There is a God who loves the world, a Christ who died for the world, and believers who are to serve the world in response to what God did through Christ.

This service is the essence of Azariah's ministry, the parable of the good Samaritan, Gandhi's quote on the archway, and Jesus' final exam. For all of us, someone nearby is hungry, thirsty, lonely, oppressed, or in need. Our genuine love for Jesus is measured by Jesus according to the offering of love we give to one in need. Like faith at work, it is wonderfully simple and obvious.

In effect, the love that we want to send "upstairs" (through worship, offering, and praise) must be in direct proportion to the love we extend down here in service to those all around us. With God there is no dichotomy between upstairs and downstairs; it is all God's domain. Therefore, God is just as intent that our love go sideways (horizontal) as upwards (vertical).

Clyde Tilley's excellent study of The Sermon on the Mount, *The Surpassing Righteousness,* helps explain God's universal concern. In dealing with Jesus' statement, "Do not swear at all, either by heaven . . . or by the earth. . . . Let your word be 'Yes, yes or No, no' " (Matt 5:34, 36, 37), Tilley explains:

> (Jesus') primary point seems to be that since God is sovereign and all-pervasive, there is nothing by which one can swear. There is nothing in which God is not involved. Consequently, this marks a defiance of our traditional compartmentalization of things into secular and sacred. Secularism de-compartmentalizes by saying that all is secular; the law of the kingdom asserts that there can be no compartmentalizing because all is sacred. This is sometimes called a sacramental view of the universe. It means that all is at God's disposal for revelation and gracious dealings with humankind.[6]

Tilley gives the perfect summary of faith at work. We can make no divisions of our activities, for God is a part of everything; therefore, all is sacred. There is no such thing as company time, personal time, free time, or fun time. All of time beongs to God. God gives us the freedom to use some time to work for the company, pursue personal interests, or have fun. God never surrenders ownership of time, however. As Tilley said, "There is nothing in which God is not involved." Jesus made it even clearer in the Sermon on the Mount passage that states,

> No one can serve two masters; for a slave will either hate the one and love the other, or be devoted to the one and despise the other. You cannot serve God and wealth. (Matt 6:24)

We have tried so long and hard to exclude God from the workplace and most other places and to confine God to worship, church, and a few charitable acts. Putting our faith to work can set us free from the division and tension that comes from serving two or more masters. Jesus said in Matthew 6:24 that if we are constantly bouncing back and forth between loyalties, we will end up hating and despising one of them. Hating and despising are powerful, painful, and dangerous feelings. We must make a choice. Faith at work extends the invitation to choose God and live a life of consummate loyalty to God.

I have always attached extra importance to what Jesus said at the beginning of his ministry and especially at the end. Consider his first public message, given in his hometown in Nazareth. Quoting from Isaiah 61, Jesus said,

> The spirit of the Lord is upon me, because he has annointed me to bring good news to the poor. He has sent me to proclaim release to the captives and recovery of sight to the blind, to let the oppressed go free, to proclaim the year of the Lord's favor. (Luke 4:18-19)

Then Jesus added, to the dismay of everyone, "Today this scripture has been fulfilled in your hearing" (v. 21). With this statement, he aligned himself squarely in the tradition of the prophets who, speaking at God's urging, wanted things changed. The prophets were never friends of the status quo nor smug and content with the way things were. For the prophets and Jesus, there was always room for improvement.

Jesus made it clear that his intention was to shake up the existing order that always seemed to leave many people at a disadvantage. The poor, the prisoners, the blind, and the oppressed were to be the focus and beneficiaries of Jesus' action. Anyone who wished to follow Jesus had to share the same focus, a full-time calling.

Skip three years to the end of Jesus' life. I have always assumed that whatever a person would choose to say at the end of life, especially if the person knew the end was coming, would be particularly important. Jesus certainly knew that his time on earth was almost over. He had precious little time left to convey to the disciples the essence of his teachings.

Near the end, Jesus gathered the disciples for an evening filled with symbolism. Often overlooked and particularly important was Jesus' determination to wash the feet of the disciples. Afterward, Jesus told them,

> So if I, your Lord and Teacher, have washed your feet, you also ought to wash one another's feet. For I have set you an example, that you also should do as I have done to you. . . . If you know these things, you are blessed if you do them. (John 13:14, 15, 17)

Jesus continued with the same theme in chapters thirteen to seventeen.

> I give you a new commandment that you love one another. Just as I have loved you, you also should love one another. By this everyone will know that you are my disciples, if you have love one for another. (John 13:34-35)

> I tell you, the one who believes in me will also do the works that I do and will do greater works than these. (John 14:12)

> This is my commandment that you love one another as I have loved you. No one has greater love than this, to lay down one's life for one's friends. You are my friends if you do what I command you. (John 15:12-14)

Soon, Jesus was betrayed, arrested, tried, and executed. Yet, he came back to live for a brief encounter to emphasize the priorities of God's kingdom. To Peter, he said not once, not twice, but three times, "Feed my lambs" (John 21:15-17). Then, when it was time for Jesus to conclude his earthly ministry, the Gospel of Matthew tells us that the disciples were brought together for one last challenge. For centuries, Christians have called this experience The Great Commission (Matt 28:19-20). In today's vernacular, it could be The Great Job Description. These two commands certainly form the heart and soul of faith at work.

Two thousand years later, the spiritual revival that Jesus started is now a worldwide force, an earthly power of great magnitude. We have certainly done a good job of going into all nations and baptizing them, but have we made disciples? We have established churches, made members, administered sacraments, and taken offerings, but these works are not the same as discipleship and full obedience.

Discipleship implies getting people to be more like Christ. To accomplish this goal, we need to remove all compartmentalization, dichotomy, confusion about two masters, and impediments to a life lived at the edge of the cross. We must teach people what Jesus commanded: living a life permeated with God's spirit, a life fully committed to God's kingdom.

Discipleship is a life of receiving communion and giving foot washings, of going into the closet to pray and picking up the cross to follow, of keeping the law and breaking the Sabbath to help a person in need, of being baptized and doing the things that lead to persecution, of being born again and being peacemakers, and of believing on the Lord Jesus Christ and feeding the hungry.

At the beginning of Jesus' public career he promised a ministry of freedom, recovery, release, and Good News for all in desperate need. By the end of his life, Jesus was crystal clear that the only way to follow in his footsteps was through a life of unqualified service and love.

We are to go into all of the world, discipling, baptizing, and building a community of people who claim the name of Christ and then live the life of Christ. This worldwide community is to do all that Jesus commanded, and above all act in service and love. These ideals are to be taught by example.

Following Jesus' commands is the center of faith at work. It seeks to give purpose and direction to all aspects of our spiritual life. It is not to the exclusion of the sacraments, piety, or ritual, but it is the follow-through. Because God first loved us, because we are baptized and born again, and because we do Communion/Lord's Supper in remembrance of Christ who died on the cross for us, we commit to a life of service and love.

Many years ago I met two older missionary ladies in Zaire. One was from England, and the other was from Australia. They both worked in lower Zaire, the center for much rebellion against the oppressive regime of President Mobutu. The rebellion, unfortunately, included indiscriminate killing and one large massacre of missionaries, co-workers, and families. Yet these missionary women were determined to return to the area to continue a life of love and service, no matter how dangerous or what the cost. When I asked them why, they simply quoted lines from a familiar hymn by Isaac Watts:

When I survey the wondrous cross
On which the Prince of Glory died
Love so amazing, so divine
Demands my soul, my life, my all.[7]

When we really consider the extent of God's love, we are compelled to respond with a tremendous, all-encompassing commitment. As we look at the cross we simply cannot be satisfied by responding, "Thank you, Jesus. Because of what you did for me I promise to attend church from time to time, take communion occasionally, get baptized once in my life, and be spiritually-minded most Sunday mornings."

If we truly believe the depth of God's love we must find ourselves saying: "Love so amazing, so divine, demands my soul, my life, my all." Love so amazing, so divine demands our tools and resources; our every effort and energy; and our work, play, and worship. This kind of love demands that we live our beliefs in practical and everyday ways.

Everyone is committed to something. Some people are committed to doing nothing, and they do it quite well! Others are committed to being half-hearted, and they succeed! Yet, some persons choose a cause or purpose.

Recently there has been an increase in interest in Malcolm X, a leader in the struggle for freedom and dignity among African-Americans. His slogan, "By Any Means Necessary," appears on tee-shirts and posters and has been taken up as a rallying cry for people seeking justice. A member of my son's baseball team wore a shirt that promises, "Whatever It Takes."

One slogan seeks justice; the other seeks a baseball championship. Both are worthwhile goals requiring maximum effort. No one can overcome oppression by taking the easy way or win a championship with a half-hearted effort. Persons who would affirm the idea of faith at work need to borrow freely from both slogans. In a world of need among the people of Christ, there are no limits, boundaries, nor compartments. The call to love and service is "By Any Means Necessary, Whatever It Takes."

Persons who take seriously a faith at work and true discipleship may face loss of job security, rejection by others, questioning from traditional religious groups, and failure. But truly committed people who want to make a difference, feel involved, be part of something that is useful, and experience practical and personal Christianity will take the risks.

The good Samaritan did not solve the problem of street crime in the ancient world, but he sure could figure out what to do for the one man he found lying in the street. Habitat for Humanity cannot keep pace with all the houses destroyed by wars and natural disasters, but it certainly can make a difference neighborhood by neighborhood. The Fire Tender could not bring rain to end the famine in Africa, but he definitely knew what to do with one empty lot to feed 1,000 hungry folks. Gandhi could not straighten out the British Empire or end the blood feud between Hindus and Moslems, but he knew how to measure every step so that one person was helped. Jesus did not stop the world from sinning and abusing, but he could look at us from the cross and say, "This is what I am doing for you." Faith at work is one way of looking at Christ and saying, "This is what we are doing for you."

Endnotes

[1]"Doing Good is Good for Business," *USA Today*, 10 June 1992, D1.

[2]Tony Edacheriparambil, *God-Concept in Gitanjali* (Bangalore India: Claretian Publications, 1990) 1.

[3]Joseph Kolagaden, foreword, ibid., 3.

[4]Ibid.

[5]David Johnson Rowe, *Something Small for God* (Hyderabad India: Prabodha Books, 1992) 33-34.

[6]Clyde Tilley, *The Surpassing Righteousness* (Macon GA: Smyth & Helwys, 1992) 95-96.

[7]Isaac Watts, "When I Survey the Wondrous Cross," 1707.

—Epilogue—

My greatest fear is that faith at work may be seen as a spiritual excuse for workaholism. The use of parallel biblical quotations and stories of Gandhi, Azariah, the Fire Tender, building houses, and feeding the hungry could lead to a guilt trip. The inevitable result of guilt-driven workaholism is burnout. Well intentioned charitable efforts have left behind a tired army of burned-out do-gooders.

Faith at work is not saying, "The world stinks, so you better try harder, give more, work better." Rather, the concept implies that with the promise of God permeating our lives we will have more joy, not less. We have all met hard workers who are miserable: neighborhood coaches, sacrificial volunteers, devoted church-goers, and obsessive parents. Faith at work fails if it only makes such people feel twice as miserable or enlists twice as many people to be just as miserable.

Faith at work only suggests that if every act and activity of our daily lives is consecrated to God, then a whole new spirit enters into every effort we make. That spirit of love and service will transform our attitude in all that we do.

Clyde Tilley says that "all is sacred." If that is too lofty a concept then try Gandhi's version:

> "Mr. Gandhi," a western journalist asked once, "you have been working at least fifteen hours a day, everyday, for almost fifty years. Don't you think it's about time you took a vacation?"
> "Why?" Gandhi said. "I am always on vacation."[1]

Gandhi offered a refreshing view of life—a living, breathing, practical, obvious theology. All that we do can be fun and exhilarating. All that we do can be an offering to God. Our life's work, elevated to a sacred vacation, shakes loose the curse of feeling that it is drudgery, routine, or punishment.

The folk group of Peter, Paul, and Mary made famous a song by Pete Seeger, "If I Had a Hammer." The first three verses tell what the singer would do if there was a hammer, a bell, or a song available with which to alert the world to the dangers of a world without love. The fourth verse is a positive affirmation of the ability each of us has to change the world.

Well I got a hammer
And I got a bell
And I got a song to sing all over this land.
It's the hammer of justice,
It's the bell of freedom,
It's the song about love between my brothers and my sisters,
All over this land.[2]

All over this land there is a need for hammers, bells, songs, soup la-
dles, helping hands, and tender touches. When these resources and God's
opportunities come together, it is not work but vacation on sacred time.

Endnotes

[1]Eknath Easwaran, *Gandhi the Man* (Nilgiri Press, 1978).
[2]Pete Seeger, "If I Had a Hammer" (New York: Ludlow Music, 1962).